ROC

TRIVIA QUIZ BOOK

500 ROCK TRIVIA QUESTIONS
(1950s–1980s)

*an encyclopedia of rock & roll's
trivia-information

in question/answer format*

by: Presley Love

Published by Hi-Lite Publishing Co.

email comments/corrections: <u>rocktrivia@test-prepHi.com</u>

THIRD EDITION -- Updated Printing: 2018

Love, Presley

ROCK & ROLL TRIVIA QUIZ BOOK

(128 pages)

1. Rock-&-Roll Quiz Book   I. Love, Presley   II. Title: Rock and Roll

2. Music

COVER DESIGN: *Doug Behrens*

ISBN–13: 978–1511664011

ISBN–10: 1511664010

Printed In The United States of America

----

text collection by: **Presley Love**

format/production by: Raymond Karelitz

The Legacy of Presley Love

In 1992, music-aficionado Presley Love compiled a vast treasure of rock and roll lyric-memoribilia, including songs from the earliest days of rock and roll up through the late '80s. This musical quiz-format collection lay dormant except for the release of one small volume, which contained 400 questions. The original book — printed in 1992 — became, over the years, an Amazon.com favorite, with very positive response from those who loved the book for its "party-flavor" appeal.

In 2014, the entire vault of Presley Love's music-lyric memoribilia was located in a storage locker — containing his collection of lyric-questions and trivia questions in quiz format! It has taken 2 years of diligent compiling and organizing to create what amounts to the entire Presley Love collection of rock lyrics, rock titles and rock group trivia books in quiz-format!

We are proud to unveil the first two books of this rare and collectible series: *PARTY ROCK LYRICS & TITLES QUIZ BOOK* and *ROCK TRIVIA QUIZ BOOK.* We sincerely hope you enjoy these fabulous party-favorites in quiz-format, a preview of the exciting treasure trove of rock & roll memories from Presley Love's truly incredible 1955-1989 collection!

If you're brave enough to test your skills,
here's a simple SCORING CHART:

(questions are worth 1 point each — "Harder Questions"
are worth 2 points each . . . If you are able to correctly
answer the question without the three choices, you
receive twice the point value!)

If you score . . .

25+ Points: You probably STILL think it's 1967!
(Check your wardrobe!)

20-24: You probably paid more attention to
rock & roll than books & school!
(Check your report card!)

15-19: There's a lot of rock & roll memories
in your blood!

10-14: Don't you wish you'd listened more closely
to rock & roll ?!
(It's never too late to be hip!)

0-9: Where were YOU when rock began to rule ?!
*(Time to get experienced —
run to your music store now!!!)*

ROCK TRIVIA QUESTIONS

1. Who said: "People like Elvis Presley were the builders of rock n' roll, but I was the architect."

        a. Chuck Berry

        b. Fats Domino

        c. Little Richard

****

2. Who is the oldest solo artist to have a Top 10 hit ?

        a. Louis Armstrong

        b. Walter Brennan

        c. Bing Crosby

****

3. Which of the following was not a member of the New Christy Minstrels ?

        a. Barry McGuire

        b. Stephen Stills

        c. Gene Clark

****

4. How did teen sensation Frankie Lymon die ?

        a. in a plane crash

        b. he was struck by lightning

        c. from a drug overdose

****

5. Otha Ellas McDaniel was the real (birth) name for which of the following ?

        a. Bo Diddley

        b. Chuck Berry

        c. Gene McDaniel

6. Who wrote the Crystals hit *He's a Rebel* ?
   - a. Hal David
   - b. Gene Pitney
   - c. Jerry Leiber and Mike Stoller

****

7. Who inspired Paul Anka's song *Diana* ?
   - a. his babysitter
   - b. his older sister
   - c. his algebra teacher

****

8. What group did producer Phil Spector originally sing for ?
   - a. the Cadets
   - b. the Teddy Bears
   - c. the Serendipity Singers

****

9. What was the first gold record recognized by the Recording Industry of America (R.I.A.A.) ?
   - a. *All Shook Up*
   - b. *Catch a Falling Star*
   - c. *Love Letters in the Sand*

****

10. What did Jackie Wilson die from ?
   - a. a stroke
   - b. lung cancer
   - c. a falling tree

11. What was Elvis Presley's debut hit on RCA Records ?
   a. *Hound Dog*
   b. *Love Me Tender*
   c. *Heartbreak Hotel*

****

12. *Linda,* a hit for Jan & Dean in 1963, was written in the '40s for a now well-known rocker. Who is she ?
   a. Linda Ronstadt
   b. Belinda Carlisle
   c. Linda Eastman

****

13. Ernest Evans was the real (birth) name for which of the following singers ?
   a. Eddie Cochran
   b. Ernie K-Doe
   c. Chubby Checker

****

14. Who was the first black American rock & roll group to top the British charts ?
   a. Frankie Lymon & The Teenagers
   b. The Drifters
   c. The Olympics

****

15. What was the first #1 Motown hit ?
   a. *My Guy* / Mary Wells
   b. *Please Mr. Postman* / Marvelettes
   c. *Money* / Barrett Strong

16. Charles Westover was the real (birth) name for which of the following rock stars ?

    a. Del Shannon

    b. Bobby Vee

    c. Fabian

****

17. Who recorded with the earliest Beach Boys but was then trimmed from their lineup shortly after their first album ?

    a. David Marks

    b. Al Jardine

    c. Bruce Johnston

****

18. Who wrote the Connie Francis hit *Where the Boys Are* ?

    a. Neil Sedaka

    b. Lesley Gore

    c. Carole King

****

19. What song was featured in an episode of *The Flintstones*, a song that actually charted in the Top 100 by Pebbles & Bamm-Bamm ?

    a. *Love Is for the Young at Heart*

    b. *It's A Small World After All*

    c. *Let the Sunshine In*

****

20. Walden Robert Cassoto was the real (birth) name for which of the following '60s stars ?

    a. Tony Orlando

    b. Bob Dylan

    c. Bobby Darin

HARDER QUESTIONS: Worth 2 points each — 4 points if you can answer the question without the three choices !

****

1. Who was the *Mr. Lee,* the focus of the Bobbettes hit single ?

      a. their high school principal

      b. their babysitter

      c. their next-door neighbor

****

2. Which musical group was originally the vocal group on "The Andy Williams Show" on television ?

      a. the New Christy Minstrels

      b. the Osmonds

      c. the Lettermen

****

3. Who played piano on the Chiffons hit *He's So Fine* ?

      a. Burt Bacharach

      b. Billy Preston

      c. Carole King

****

4. Who gave up his seat to The Big Bopper on the ill-fated airplane which took the lives of Buddy Holly, The Big Bopper and Ritchie Valens ?

      a. Ricky Nelson

      b. Waylon Jennings

      c. Dion

****

5. How did Jay & the Americans get their name ?

    a. Jay was named for Jay Black, their lead singer

    b. Jay was the nickname of John Traynor, the original lead singer of the group

    c. the name "Jay" sounded good with "Americans"

ANSWERS

****

1. c. Little Richard
2. b. Walter Brennan (Famous as Grandpa in *The Real McCoys*, he was 67 years old when he hit #5 with his 1962 hit *Old Rivers*.)
3. b. Stephen Stills
4. c. from a drug overdose (in 1968)
5. a. Bo Diddley
6. b. Gene Pitney
7. a. his babysitter
8. b. The Teddy Bears (including their 1958 hit *To Know Him Is To Love Him*, which he wrote)
9. b. *Catch a Falling Star* (Perry Como hit in 1958)
10. a. a stroke (he was stricken in 1975 while performing on stage at the Latin Casino in New Jersey—he passed away in 1984, after many years in the hospital)
11. c. *Heartbreak Hotel*
12. c. Linda Eastman (later to be Mrs. Linda McCartney)
13. c. Chubby Checker
14. a. Frankie Lymon & The Teenagers (in August, 1956 with *Why Do Fools Fall in Love*)
15. b. *Please Mr. Postman* / Marvelettes (#1 in December, 1961)
16. a. Del Shannon
17. a. David Marks (a neighbor of the Hawthorne, California, band)
18. a. Neil Sedaka
19. c. *Let the Sunshine In* (full title: *Open Up Your Heart and Let the Sunshine In*)
20. c. Bobby Darin

****

HARDER QUESTIONS--Answers

1. a. their high school principal (although another report says he was their 5th grade teacher)
2. a. The New Christy Minstrels
3. c. Carole King
4. b. Waylon Jennings (who was at that time a member of Buddy Holly's backup group, the Crickets...Tommy Allsup, the Crickets' guitarist, gave up his seat to Ritchie Valens)
5. b. Jay was the nickname of John Traynor, the original lead singer of the group. (According to co-founder Kenny Vance, Jerry Lieber originally wanted to call them Binky Jones & the Americans, but John Traynor's nickname met with more approval by the band than did Binky Jones. "Americans" came as from Lieber's "amazing imagination"—he had a plane ticket on his desk from American Airlines, and presto came the name!)

1. Jan & Dean's first hit, *Jennie Lee,* was recorded under the moniker Jan & Arnie. Who was Jennie Lee and who was Arnie ?

   a. Jennie Lee was a teacher; Arnie was Jan's brother.
   b. Jennie Lee was a '40s movie star; Arnie was Dean's alias.
   c. Jennie Lee was a stripper; Arnie was a friend of Jan's.

****

2. Who gave Chubby Checker his stage-name ?

   a. Fats Domino
   b. Dick Clark's wife
   c. Berry Gordy

****

3. Who sang backup vocals on Sam Cooke's hit *Bring It On Home To Me* ?

   a. Lou Rawls
   b. Nat "King" Cole
   c. Otis Redding

****

4. In which of the following songs is the title word <u>not</u> mentioned ?

   a. *Wipeout* / Surfaris
   b. *Tequila* / Champs
   c. *Sukiyaki* / Kyu Sakamoto

****

5. Who did Jerry Lee Lewis marry in 1958, an event which severley damaged his music career ?

   a. his thirteen-year-old cousin
   b. his manager's daughter
   c. an avowed atheist

6. How did early rock star Johnny Ace die ?

  a. in a train crash

  b. by playing Russian roulette

  c. in a blood-transfusion medical mishap

****

7. Who was the actual non-Crystals lead singer on the Crystals' hit *He's a Rebel* ?

  a. Martha Reeves

  b. Shirley Jackson

  c. Darlene Love

****

8. Which Beach Boys song featured cheerleading ?

  a. *Be True to Your School*

  b. *When I Grow Up (To Be a Man)*

  c. *Heroes and Villains*

****

9. What group did the Primettes later become ?

  a. The Ikettes

  b. The Shangri-Las

  c. The Supremes

****

10. What controversial movie did *Rock Around the Clock* first appear in that resulted in a #1 hit for Bill Haley & His Comets ?

  a. *Go Johnny Go!*

  b. *Blackboard Jungle*

  c. *Rock Around the Clock*

11. Only one Jan & Dean song ever reached #1.
    Which song was it ?
    a. *Surf City*
    b. *The Little Old Lady From Pasadena*
    c. *Dead Man's Curve*

****

12. What is *Puff The Magic Dragon* a song about ?
    a. a bad drug trip
    b. a fairy tale involving a dragon
    c. the short life of fame and success

****

13. Where was Elvis Presley born ?
    a. Tupelo, Mississippi
    b. Memphis, Tennessee
    c. Nashville, Tennessee

****

14. In *Big Bad John,* the last line of the song was changed
    to "At the bottom of this mine lies a big, big man".
    What was the original final line in the original release,
    before it was pulled and replaced ?
    a. "At the bottom of this mine lies a true American".
    b. "At the bottom of this mine lies one helluva man".
    c. "At the bottom of this mine is the future of mankind".

****

15. Who sang the lead on the Beach Boys' hit *Barbara Ann* ?
    a. Brian Wilson
    b. Mike Love
    c. Dean Torrence

16. What was the original name of the Marketts hit instrumental *Out of Limits* ?

    a. *Twilight Zone*

    b. *Outer Limits*

    c. *One Step Beyond*

****

17. What was Elvis Presley's middle name ?

    a. Mitchell

    b. Aron

    c. Samuel

****

18. What song was released as an answer to Gene Chandler's 1962 hit *The Duke of Earl* ?

    a. *The Duchess of Earl*

    b. *Walking With the Duke*

    c. *I Married the Duke of Earl*

****

19. With which group did Neil Sedaka sing early in his career ?

    a. the Diamonds

    b. the Chipmunks

    c. the Tokens

****

20. What was the Beach Boys' first #1 hit ?

    a. *I Get Around*

    b. *Surfin' U.S.A.*

    c. *Help Me, Rhonda*

HARDER QUESTIONS: Worth 2 points each — 4 points if you can answer the question without the three choices !

****

1. Who played the guitar solo on the Drifters' *On Broadway* ?
   - a. Phil Spector
   - b. Bill Withers
   - c. George Benson

****

2. Which famous solo artist was among the backup singers on *Da Doo Ron Ron* (Crystals) and *Be My Baby* (Ronettes) ?
   - a. Diana Ross
   - b. Mary Wells
   - c. Cher

****

3. Who recorded *Only In America* just prior to Jay & the Americans' version ?
   - a. the Drifters
   - b. Jack Jones
   - c. the Four Seasons

****

4. What made Phil Spector recording sessions quite unique ?
   - a. he never re-hired the same back-up musicians
   - b. he never recorded at night
   - c. he never recorded the sessions in stereo

****

5. What was the Bobbettes' follow-up song to *Mr. Lee* ?
   - a. *Jivin' With Mr. Lee*
   - b. *The Future Mrs. Lee*
   - c. *I Shot Mr. Lee*

ANSWERS

****

1. c. Jennie Lee was a stripper; Arnie (Ginsberg) was a friend of Jan's (and early group member).
2. b. Dick Clark's wife (it was a humorous takeoff on "Fats Domino")
3. a. Lou Rawls
4. c. *Sukiyaki* /Kyu Sakamoto
5. a. his thirteen-year-old cousin
6. b. by playing Russian roulette (on Christmas Eve, 1954)
7. c. Darlene Love (along with her group The Blossoms...As recalled by Darlene Love, the Crystals "had a falling out" with producer Phil Spector, who wanted to have the song recorded—and because the Crystals had moved to New York while she was living in Los Angeles, the city where the studio was located, she was chosen by Spector to record the song. Incidentally, once the song became a national hit, the Crystals had to learn the song to sing on their tours!)
8. a. *Be True to Your School* (featuring the Honeys)
9. c. The Supremes
10. b. *Blackboard Jungle* (it played at the 1955 movie's introduction; the movie *Rock Around the Clock* was released in 1956)
11. a. *Surf City* (in 1963)
12. b. a fairy tale involving a dragon (Writer Peter Yarrow adamantly stated that, if he wanted to write a song about the evils of drugs, he'd have been explicit in his lyrics. As he once commented: "Puff is a dragon and drugs are drugs, and never the twain shall meet...until you can show me a junkie dragon".)
13. a. Tupelo, Mississippi
14. b. "At the bottom of this mine lies one helluva man".
15. c. Dean Torrence (of Jan & Dean) (Dean Torrence walked into the Beach Boys' studio during a break, suggested the song, and then joined the group during the Beach Boys' *Party* album's recording. Due to label conflicts, Dean was not credited for his lead vocals.)
16. b. *Outer Limits* (Due to the popularity of a new weekly sci-fi program titled *The Outer Limits*—to which the song had no affiliation—it didn't take long for the Warner Brothers record company to make the necessary change.)
17. b. Elvis Aron Presley
18. a. *The Duchess of Earl* (1962) by the Pearlettes
19. c. the Tokens
20. a. *I Get Around* (1964)

****

HARDER QUESTIONS—Answers

1. a. Phil Spector
2. c. Cher
3. a. the Drifters (As Jay & the Americans co-founder Kenny Vance tells it, "1963...was a different time in America" and a black group singing about getting a break "to become President" just wasn't realistic or even acceptable. So their version was produced and released instead, adding their vocals to the original instrumental track.)
4. c. he never recorded the sessions in stereo . . . (editor note: I've recently heard a stereo version of *Uptown*, so I am a bit baffled...perhaps only Phil Spector knows for sure)
5. c. *I Shot Mr. Lee*

1. What is Lou Christie's real (birth) name ?
   a. Lewis Cianni
   b. Lugee Sacco
   c. Antonio Massi

****

2. Which of the following young stars did <u>not</u> perform their own Top 20 Single hit on a family-favorite weekly television show ?
   a. Shelley Fabares singing *Johnny Angel*
   b. Paul Petersen singing *My Dad*
   c. Johnny Crawford singing *Cindy's Birthday*

****

3. Which Top 10 Beach Boys hit was actually an adaptation of a Chuck Berry hit ?
   a. *Barbara Ann*
   b. *Surfin' U.S.A.*
   a. *Sloop John B*

****

4. Who was the lead singer for all five of the Platters' million-selling records ?
   a. Sonny Turner
   b. Linda Hayes
   c. Tony Williams

****

5. Which rock & roll singer is the cousin of famed television evangelist Jimmy Swaggart ?
   a. Jerry Lee Lewis
   b. Johnny Tillotson
   c. Bobby Rydell

6. Little Eva had a smash hit in 1962 with Carole King's composition *The Loco-Motion.* Who was Little Eva ?

    a. Carole King's neighbor

    b. Carole King's babysitter

    c. The daughter of Carole King's manager

****

7. Which of the following songs does <u>not</u> contain the exact words as in the song's title ?

    a. *Pony Time* / Chubby Checker

    b. *Dedicated to the One I Love* / Shirelles

    c. *He Will Break Your Heart* / Jerry Butler

****

8. Gary Puckett was born in Hibbing, Minnesota. What legendary rock figure had his earliest roots in that area ?

    a. Chuck Berry

    b. Elvis Presley

    c. Bob Dylan

****

9. Who was the original manager of the Beatles ?

    a. Brian Epstein

    b. Mickie Most

    c. George Martin

****

10. William Howard Ashton was the real (birth) name for which of the following ?

    a. Bill Medley

    b. Billy J. Kramer

    c. Eric Burdon

11. What was the name of the '60s band that Van Morrison was leader singer for ?

> a. Music Explosion
> b. Music Machine
> c. Them

****

12. In what world–televised live event did Who's drummer Keith Moon perform in 1967 ?

> a. the Rolling Stones' Royal Albert Hall performance
> b. the 1967 Grammy Awards, with the Yardbirds
> c. the Beatles *All You Need is Love* recording session

****

13. In what year was Herman's Hermits #1 hit
I'm Henry VIII I Am written ?

> a. 1911
> b. 1953
> c. 1962

****

14. Why did the Byrds select the unusual spelling for their name ?

> a. to poke fun at the movie *Bye Bye Birdie*
> b. so as not to be confused with "birds," a British slang for "girls"
> c. to express their allegiance to Bob Dylan

****

15. In what newspaper did an ad appear seeking four guys to form the Monkees ?

> a. *Rolling Stone*
> b. *Hollywood Reporter*
> c. *Wall Street Journal*

16. Just before Jan Berry crashed his Corvette and was nearly killed, what news had he received ?

       a. that he was accepted into U.C.L.A.

       b. that he had excelled on the SAT

       c. that he was soon to be drafted

****

17. From what country did the Troggs come ?

       a. England

       b. Holland

       c. Canada

****

18. Under what group name were Jefferson Airplane's first hits, *Somebody to Love* and *White Rabbit,* originally recorded ?

       a. the Slick Stick

       b. the Where

       c. the Great Society

****

19. How did Herman's Hermits get their name ?

   a. The group members lived like hermits.

   b. Leader Peter Noone resembled googly-eyed Sherman on *The Bullwinkle Show.*

   c. It was patterned after a local female group, Merna's Mermaids.

****

20. Who was the lead singer of the Dave Clark Five ?

       a. Mike Smith

       b. Dennis Payton

       c. Dave Clark

HARDER QUESTIONS: Worth 2 points each — 4 points if you can answer the question without the three choices !

****

1. When did the name Shondells come to mind for Tommy James as a good name for his group ?
   - a. at his junior prom
   - b. during a date with a girl named Shonda
   - c. during study hall in the seventh grade

****

2. Who did the Kinks begin as, prior to their more popular name ?
   - a. the Beginners
   - b. the Hedgehoppers
   - c. the Ravens

****

3. Before joining the Mamas & the Papas, what was Mama Cass working as ?
   - a. an actress
   - b. a waitress
   - c. a teacher

****

4. The Rolling Stones hit *Play With Fire* was credited to the writer Nanker Phelge. Who was he ?
   - a. a pseudonym for Mick Jagger/Keith Richards
   - b. the band's first manager
   - c. Mick Jagger's uncle

****

5. Mary O'Brien was the real (birth) name for which of the following British stars ?
   - a. Petula Clark
   - b. Dusty Springfield
   - c. Mary Hopkin

ANSWERS

****

1. b. Lugee Sacco
2. c. Johnny Crawford singing *Cindy's Birthday* (As the son of Lucas McCain on *The Rifleman,* he was not given the chance to showcase his hits, as were Shelley Fabares and Paul Petersen, who each had their television moment during two different episodes of *The Donna Reed Show.* Of course, Johnny Crawford did perform in dozens of concerts and had several Top 20 hits in the early '60s...The most musically fortunate '60s child star of all, by the way, was Ricky Nelson (later, Rick Nelson) who had the ideal platform to play his hits week after week on *The Ozzie and Harriet Show.*)
3. b. *Surfin' U.S.A.* (adapted from Chuck Berry's *Sweet Little Sixteen*)
4. c. Tony Williams
5. a. Jerry Lee Lewis
6. b. Carole King's babysitter
7. c. *He Will Break Your Heart* / Jerry Butler (the refrain is: "He don't love you like I love you—if he did he wouldn't break your heart. He don't love you like I love you—he's trying to tear us apart".)
8. c. Bob Dylan (who attended Hibbing High School)
9. a. Brian Epstein
10. b. Billy J. Kramer
11. c. Them
12. c. the Beatles *All You Need is Love* recording session—recorded live as part of a satellite TV–airing
13. a. 1911
14. b. so as not to be confused with "birds", a British slang for "girls"
15. b. *Hollywood Reporter*
16. c. that he was soon to be drafted
17. a. England
18. c. the Great Society
19. b. Leader Peter Noone resembled googly–eyed Sherman on *The Bullwinkle Show.* The group took advantage of the similarity to call themselves Herman & His Hermits, later Herman's Hermits...Sherman's Shermits wouldn't have worked out as well!
20. a. Mike Smith (Dave Clark was the drummer)

****

HARDER QUESTIONS--Answers

1. c. during study hall in the seventh grade
2. c. the Ravens
3. b. a waitress
4. a. a pseudonym for Mick Jagger/Keith Richards
5. b. Dusty Springfield

1. What famous street corner is associated with the earliest days of the Jefferson Airplane ?
   - a. Hollywood and Vine
   - b. Haight and Ashbury
   - c. Sunset and Wilshire

****

2. In what year was the Zombies' last hit, *Time of the Season,* recorded ?
   - a. 1965
   - b. 1967
   - c. 1969

****

3. In what TV series did Monkees singer Micky Dolenz appear as a youngster ?
   - a. *Gilligan's Island*
   - b. *Ben Casey*
   - c. *Circus Boy*

****

4. Who co-wrote the Searchers' first U.S. hit, *Needles & Pins,* with Jack Nitzsche ?
   - a. Sonny Bono
   - b. Del Shannon
   - c. Paul Simon

****

5. What song did Wings' member Denny Laine sing lead on, a 1965 hit for a legendary British group he helped form ?
   - a. *Double Shot (of My Baby's Love)*
   - b. *She's Not There*
   - c. *Go Now*

6. From what book did the Doors get their group's name ?
>   a. *The Doors of Perception*
>   b. *Unlocking the Doors of the Imagination*
>   c. *Through the Doors of Time*

****

7. What was Bob Dylan's birth name ?
>   a. Robert Weberman
>   b. Robert Zimmerman
>   c. Robert Weisberg

****

8. Where was the Left Banke from ?
>   a. Manchester, England
>   b. Sydney, Australia
>   c. New York, U.S.A.

****

9. Before leading the Rolling Stones, what band did Mick Jagger sing for ?
>   a. Blues Incorporated
>   b. the London Boys
>   c. the Edge of Tyme

****

10. Who played lead guitar on Them's hit *Gloria* ?
>   a. Jimmy Page
>   b. Van Morrison
>   c. Glen Campbell

11. What was the Beatles' first #1 hit in the USA ?

> a. *She Loves You*
> b. *Love Me Do*
> c. *I Want to Hold Your Hand*

****

12. The Searchers' first drummer, Norman McGarry, left the group to join the band Rory Storm & the Hurricanes, replacing their drummer who had also switched groups. Which drummer did McGarry replace ?

> a. Keith Moon
> b. Charlie Watts
> c. Ringo Starr

****

13. Which well-known guitarist actually helped Herman's Hermits in the recording of *I'm Into Something Good* ?

> a. Jimmy Page
> b. Rick Derringer
> c. Paul McCartney

****

14. How did the Hollies get their name ?

> a. They were named during the Christmas season.
> b. They were inspired by Buddy Holly.
> c. They formed in Holland.

****

15. With which record label did the Turtles record all their '60s hits ?

> a. White Whale
> b. ABC-Paramount
> c. Jubilee

16. What was the Association's biggest hit ?

      a. *Windy*

      b. *Cherish*

      c. *Never My Love*

****

17. In which city did the Monkees perform their first live show ?

      a. San Francisco

      b. Honolulu

      c. Anaheim

****

18. What underground classic did the Rolling Stones record (but never release) to complete a contract deal with Decca Records ?

      a. *Hold on Cocaine*

      b. *Decca the Halls*

      c. *Cocksucker Blues*

****

19. What incident abruptly halted the success of Gary Lewis & the Playboys ?

      a. his father Jerry's hosting of the MDA (Muscular Dystrophy Association) telethon

      b. Gary Lewis' induction into the army

      c. the "British Invasion"

****

20. How did singer Otis Redding die ?

      a. in a plane crash

      b. he was shot by a crazed fan

      c. in a house fire

HARDER QUESTIONS: Worth 2 points each — 4 points if you can answer the question without the three choices !

****

1. Which of the following were the Turtles <u>not</u> known as ?
>   a. the Nightriders
>   b. the Undivided Sum
>   c. the Crossfires

****

2. What is the significance of the name "Jefferson Airplane" ?
   a. It was the name of a friend's dog.
   b. It was a World War I fighter plane.
   c. It combined their favorite president and a mode of travel.

****

3. Which famous child star (and former original Mousketeer) was a member of the '60s group Yellow Balloon, who had their brief moment of fame with their eponymous 1967 hit ?
>   a. Johnny Crawford/"The Rifleman"
>   b. Don Grady/"My Three Sons"
>   c. Paul Petersen/"The Donna Reed Show"

****

4. Who wrote the Peter & Gordon '60s hit *I Go To Pieces* ?
>   a. Engelbert Humperdinck
>   b. John Lennon and Paul McCartney
>   c. Del Shannon

****

5. What was Mitch Ryder's birth name ?
>   a. William Levise, Jr.
>   b. Conrad Mitchell Rydell
>   c. Mitchell Ryder Bernstein

ANSWERS

****

1. b. Haight and Ashbury
2. b. 1967 (It was released in 1969, when "the time was right." Oddly, the group had already disbanded, way back in 1967!)
3. c. *Circus Boy* (billed as Mickey Braddock)
4. a. Sonny Bono
5. c. *Go Now* (as lead singer for the original Moody Blues)
6. a. *The Doors of Perception* (Aldous Huxley's book, in which "doors" are equated with drugs)
7. b. Robert Allan Zimmerman
8. c. New York
9. a. Blues Incorporated
10. a. Jimmy Page
11. c. *I Want to Hold Your Hand* (seven weeks as #1, beginning in January, 1964)
12. c. Ringo Starr (who made the switch to replace recently-fired Pete Best in another popular local band: the Beatles)
13. a. Jimmy Page (who also played the intro/outro guitar-solo in the Hermits' *Silhouettes* as well as on several other Hermits songs)
14. b. They were inspired by Buddy Holly. (Some say they were named for the Christmas Season, but Graham Nash set the record straight in a foreword he wrote in 1984.)
15. a. White Whale (as did singing duo Rene & Rene)
16. a. *Windy* (#1 for four weeks in 1967)
17. b. Honolulu (in late 1966)
18. c. *Cocksucker Blues*
19. b. Gary Lewis' induction into the army (in January 1967)
20. a. in a plane crash (in 1967)

****

HARDER QUESTIONS--Answers

1. b. the Undivided Sum
2. a. It was the name of a friend's dog. It is also slang for a marijuana roach-clip, but the group credits four-legged Thomas Jefferson Airplane as their inspiration. After all, a dog—not a joint—is man's best friend. (PS: The slang term was derived from the reputation the group had acquired... however, the dog came first; the reputation followed.)
3. b. Don Grady/"My Three Sons"...Cast as Robbie Douglas, Grady was the singer and guitarist who led the California pop-music quintet—semi-anonymously credited on the album as "Luke Yoo"...! Johnny Crawford, by the way, was also a former Mousketeer.)
4. c. Del Shannon
5. a. William Levise, Jr. (the name "Mitch Ryder" was selected from a telephone directory!)

1. Who said the following: "We're more popular than Jesus now. I don't know which will go first — rock & roll or Christianity."

        a. John Lennon

        b. Mick Jagger

        c. Brian Wilson

****

2. Before forming the Lovin' Spoonful, two members belonged to a group with members who later formed another top '60s group. Who was this other group ?

        a. the Byrds

        b. Creedence Clearwater Revival

        c. the Mamas & the Papas

****

3. From what country did the Zombies' members come ?

        a. England

        b. the U.S.

        c. Australia

****

4. What television music show, produced by Dick Clark, did Paul Revere & the Raiders host from 1968 to 1969 ?

        a. *Shindig*

        b. *Where the Action Is*

        c. *Happening '68*

****

5. At what famous British club in Liverpool did the Beatles make their debut ?

        a. the Casbah Club

        b. the Star–Club

        c. the Cavern Club

6. From what did the Searchers select their group name ?

       a. a movie

       b. a TV game show

       c. a novel

****

7. Which of the following was <u>not</u> a name the Beach Boys used before their surfing name ?

       a. Kenny & the Cadets

       b. the Surfers

       c. the Pendletones

****

8. Although it never broke into the Top 40 charts, what was the Young Rascals' debut single ?

       a. *You Better Run*

       b. *I Ain't Gonna Eat Out My Heart Anymore*

       c. *It's Wonderful*

****

9. Who was the lead singer of Paul Revere & the Raiders ?

       a. Paul Revere

       b. Freddie Weller

       c. Mark Lindsay

****

10. The Rolling Stones' name was taken from a Muddy Waters song. Who first suggested the name ?

       a. Muddy Waters

       b. Brian Jones

       c. John Lennon

11. Before being names the Association, what name had they considered ?

      a. the Hexagrams

      b. the Troubadours

      c. the Aristocrats

****

12. Who was the lead singer of the band Manfred Mann ?

      a. Manfred Mann

      b. Mike Hugg

      c. Paul Jones

****

13. Who wrote *Different Drum,* the Stone Poneys' biggest hit ?

      a. Kenny Rogers

      b. Michael Nesmith

      c. Linda Ronstadt

****

14. Why was Ringo Starr missing during the mid-1964 Beatles world tour ?

    a. he was afraid of flying

    b. he was stricken with tonsillitis

    c. it was due to a contract dispute with Decca Records

****

15. The Troggs shortened their original name, the Troglodytes. What is a troglodyte ?

      a. a mythical caveman

      b. a small but voracious rodent

      c. a dental drill

16. Which well-known rocker joined the Buffalo Springfield on stage during their 1967 appearance at the Monterey Pop Festival ?
   a. Paul McCartney
   b. Jimi Hendrix
   c. David Crosby

****

17. In what U.S. movie did Herman's Hermits make a cameo appearance while first visiting the states ?
   a. *Freakout U.S.A.*
   b. *When the Boys Meet the Girls*
   c. *Bikini Beach Party*

****

18. Why did the Who abandon their original group name, the High Numbers ?
   a. "High Numbers" sounded too much like gambling.
   b. The name was considered too long.
   c. It associated the band with drugs.

****

19. What was the Byrds' last single to reach the Top 40 charts ?
   a. *So You Want to Be a Rock 'n' Roll Star*
   b. *Eight Miles High*
   c. *My Back Pages*

****

20. What instrumental '60s hit was originally made for an Alka-Seltzer commercial ?
   a. *Walk Don't Run* / Ventures
   b. *No Matter What Shape (Your Stomach's In)* / T-Bones
   c. *Wipeout* / Surfaris

HARDER QUESTIONS: Worth 2 points each — 4 points if you can answer the question without the three choices !

****

1. On what television show did the Rolling Stones make their U.S. debut appearance ?
   - a. *The Ed Sullivan Show*
   - b. *The Tonight Show*
   - c. *The Les Crane Show*

****

2. What were Mitch Ryder & the Detroit Wheels originally known as ?
   - a. the Memphis Experiment
   - b. Billy Lee & the Rivieras
   - c. the Manhattan Dimension

****

3. What inspired Procol Harum to select their group name ?
   - a. a friend's Siamese cat
   - b. a label on a designer shirt
   - c. the Vienna Boys Choir

****

4. Which group was being referred to as "a nightmare — musically they are a near-disaster . . . guitars and drums slamming out a merciless beat that does away with secondary rhythms . . . their lyrics are a catastrophe . . . of valentine-card sentiments."
   - a. Cream
   - b. the Beatles
   - c. the Rolling Stones

****

5. What were they called before naming themselves the Buckinghams ?
   - a. the Leftovers
   - b. the Pulsations
   - c. the Portraits

ANSWERS

****

1. a. John Lennon
2. c. the Mamas & the Papas (John Sebastian and Zal Yanovsky teamed with Cass Elliot and Denny Doherty as the Mugwumps, in 1964.)
3. a. England
4. c. *Happening '68* (*Where the Action Is* aired in 1965)
5. c. the Cavern Club (as the Quarrymen—Paul McCartney had not yet joined and did not perform at the debut)
6. a. a 1956 movie starring John Wayne
7. b. the Surfers
8. b. *I Ain't Gonna Eat Out My Heart Anymore* (which reached #52 in 1966)
9. c. Mark Lindsay (Paul Revere was the keyboardist)
10. b. Brian Jones
11. c. the Aristocrats (according to leader Terry Kirkman)
12. c. Paul Jones (Manfred Mann was the keyboardist)
13. b. Michael Nesmith (Monkees)
14. b. he was stricken with tonsillitis
15. a. a mythical caveman (similar to the "missing link" of evolutionary research)
16. c. David Crosby (he filled in for Neil Young, who had briefly quit the group at that time)
17. b. *When the Boys Meet the Girls*
18. a. "High Numbers" sounded too much like gambling (The term actually means "being in style," but for promotional purposes it came off more as an ad for bingo than for a rock group!)
19. c. *My Back Pages* (which reached #30 in 1967)
20. b. *No Matter What Shape (Your Stomach's In)* /T-Bones

****

HARDER QUESTIONS--Answers

1. c. *The Les Crane Show* (on June 2, 1964)
2. b. Billy Lee & the Rivieras
3. a. a friend's Siamese cat (in Latin, the words actually mean "beyond these things," for what it's worth!)
4. b. the Beatles (from a *Newsweek* cover-story on the Beatles)
5. b. the Pulsations

1. Which of the following was <u>not</u> a guitarist at one time for the Yardbirds ?
> a. Pete Townshend
> b. Eric Clapton
> c. Jimmy Page

****

2. From which early '60s group did three of the original four Young Rascals come ?
> a. the Ventures
> b. Joey Dee & the Starliters
> c. the Danleers

****

3. Which of the following songs does <u>not</u> contain the exact words as in the song's title ?
> a. *Soul & Inspiration* / Righteous Brothers
> b. *Can't You Hear My Heart Beat* / Herman's Hermits
> c. *Homeward Bound* / Simon & Garfunkel

****

4. Which well-known manager signed Billy J. Kramer & the Dakotas to a multi-year contract ?
> a. Tony Hatch
> b. Andrew Loog Oldham
> c. Brian Epstein

****

5. *(I Can't Get No) Satisfaction* was the Stones' first #1 hit. What was their last ?
> a. *Start Me Up*
> b. *Honky Tony Women*
> c. *Miss You*

6. In what country was George Ivan (Van) Morrison born ?
        a. Russia
        b. Northern Ireland
        c. Scotland

****

7. Which song by the Mamas & the Papas tells the story of their rise to rock stardom ?
        a. *Creeque Alley*
        b. *Monday, Monday*
        c. *California Dreamin'*

****

8. Which of the following names did the Beatles <u>not</u> record under ?
        a. the Quarrymen
        b. the Beatmakers
        c. the Silver Beatles

****

9. Which famous solo performer toured in 1965 as a Beach Boy when Brian Wilson quit performing ?
        a. Brian Hyland
        b. Lou Christie
        c. Glen Campbell

****

10. Why was the Kingsmen's biggest hit, *Louie, Louie* investigated by the FBI and the FCC ?
  a. it was due to a legal conflict with Paul Revere & the Raiders' version
  b. because it failed to list the band's name on the record label
  c. because of reportedly obscene lyrics

11. After what did the Buffalo Springfield name themselves ?
>   a. an Indian tribe
>   b. a rifle
>   c. a steamroller

****

12. Although popular in the U.K. long before breaking into the U.S. charts, what song finally launched the Hollies' success in the states ?
>   a. *Bus Stop*
>   b. *Carrie-Ann*
>   c. *Look Through Any Window*

****

13. What did Doors lead singer Jim Morrison allegedly do during a concert in Miami, Florida, that later got him arrested ?
>   a. he set the drums on fire
>   b. he hosted a pot party between sets
>   c. he exposed himself on stage

****

14. What did Jimi Hendrix do during the 1967 Monterey Pop Festival performance that singled him out as a truly unique audience-pleaser ?
>   a. he set his guitar on fire
>   b. he invited four spectators to join him on stage
>   c. he played his electric guitar with his toes

****

15. Who was lead singer of Herman's Hermits ?
>   a. Keith Hopwood
>   b. Peter Noone
>   c. Karl Green

16. Which Rolling Stones album featured a 3-D cover ?
> a. *Beggar's Banquet*
>
> b. *Sticky Fingers*
>
> c. *Their Satanic Majesties Request*

****

17. What is folk-rock singer Donovan's last name ?
> a. Leitch
>
> b. Spedding
>
> c. Sturdley

****

18. In what city were the Beau Brummels formed ?
> a. London
>
> b. New York City
>
> c. San Francisco

****

19. Who was the first British group to top the American charts ?
> a. the Tornadoes
>
> b. the Shadows
>
> c. the Beatles

****

20. The Turtles' name was originally suggested to be spelled differently. How did their manager want it spelled, and why ?
> a. Turttles, to match the original spelling of the Beatles' name (Beattles)
>
> b. Tyrtles, to imitate the Byrds' spelling
>
> c. Turdles, to make fun of the pop music trends

HARDER QUESTIONS: Worth 2 points each — 4 points if you can answer the question without the three choices !

****

1. Before he teamed up with the Dakotas, who was Billy J. Kramer's backup band ?

    a. the Coasters

    b. the Flagstaffers

    c. the Pennsylvanians

****

2. What Beatles song did American songwriter Jerry Leiber say was the best song ever written ?

    a. *Eleanor Rigby*

    b. *A Day in the Life*

    c. *Revolution*

****

3. Prior to becoming a Young Rascal, what song did Gene Cornish & the Unbeatables record?

    a. *I Want to Be a Beatle*

    b. *Fly Me to the Moon*

    c. *Let's Groove*

****

4. Which of the following groups was formed to raise money to help their rugby team travel to Holland for a match ?

    a. Herman's Hermits

    b. the Dave Clark Five

    c. the Hollies

****

5. What was the name of the '60s video jukebox which enjoyed only brief popularity ?

    a. Magnavision

    b. Scopitone

    c. Starbox

ANSWERS

****

1. a. Pete Townshend
2. b. Joey Dee & the Starliters (all except Dino Danelli)
3. a. *Soul & Inspiration* / Righteous Brothers (the refrain is: "You're my soul and my heart's inspiration")
4. c. Brian Epstein (manager of the Beatles)
5. c. *Miss You* (in 1978)
6. b. Northern Ireland
7. a. *Creeque Alley* (actually pronounced Cree-Kee Alley)
8. b. the Beatmakers
9. c. Glen Campbell
10. c. because of reportedly obscene lyrics (One explanation of the lyrics' cryptic nature is that they were adapted from Jamaican English, thereby creating variations on the standard pronunciation and making very ordinary lyrics sound unusual, and hence perhaps "obscene" in a subliminal way. However, obscene or not, fact is that the lyrics have never really been understandable—by American or Jamaican audiences!)
11. c. a steamroller (a sign on it read "Buffalo, Springfield")
12. a. *Bus Stop* (Though *Look Through Any Window* was their first release that broke into the U.S. charts, it was nowhere near being called a "hit".)
13. c. he exposed himself on stage
14. a. he set his guitar on fire in a bizarre ritual
15. b. Peter Noone
16. c. *Their Satanic Majesties Request*
17. a. Leitch
18. c. San Francisco (1964)
19. a. the Tornadoes (with their instrumental hit *Telstar,* which reached #1 in January, 1963)
20. b. Tyrtles, to imitate the Byrds' spelling

****

HARDER QUESTIONS--Answers

1. a. the Coasters (a local British band—not the American R&B group!)
2. a. *Eleanor Rigby*
3. a. *I Want to Be a Beatle*
4. b. Dave Clark Five
5. b. Scopitone

1. Which Top 10 Manfred Mann hit was written by
   Bob Dylan, inspired by a movie ?
          a. *Do Wah Diddy Diddy*
          b. *With God on Our Side*
          c. *The Mighty Quinn*

****

2. Which member of the original Byrds later became part
   of a highly successful trio ?
          a. Gene Clark
          b. David Crosby
          c. Chris Hillman

****

3. What was the Rascals' biggest hit, topping the charts
   for five weeks ?
          a. *People Got to Be Free*
          b. *Good Lovin'*
          c. *Groovin'*

****

4. Which song was the only #1 hit for the Dave Clark Five ?
          a. *Over & Over*
          b. *Because*
          c. *Glad All Over*

****

5. What event in Bob Dylan's life changed his musical style,
   leading to a more introspective and simple, often
   religious, focus ?
          a. a motorcycle accident
          b. a bitter divorce
          c. first hearing the Beatles *Nowhere Man* 45rpm

6. Who played lead guitar on the Beach Boys hit
   Good Vibrations ?
   > a. Al Jardine
   > b. Ron Wilson
   > c. Glen Campbell

****

7. Which song of the following did Elvis Presley sing to
   conclude each concert ?
   > a. *Can't Help Falling In Love*
   > b. *Hunk of Burnin' Love*
   > c. *Love Me Tender*

****

8. What was the Mamas & the Papas' only #1 hit ?
   > a. *Dedicated to the One I Love*
   > b. *Monday, Monday*
   > c. *California Dreamin'*

****

9. What rock classic did Van Morrison write and record
   with his '60s band ?
   > a. *Fever*
   > b. *Gloria*
   > c. *Louie, Louie*

****

10. Who wrote the Monkees hit *I'm a Believer* ?
    > a. Neil Diamond
    > b. Neil Sedaka
    > c. Peter Tork

11. What was the first rock & roll group to record under the Columbia Records label ?
    a. the Byrds
    b. Chad & Jeremy
    c. Paul Revere & the Raiders

****

12. Which of the following did not try out for (and get turned down for) the Monkees ?
    a. Sonny Bono
    b. Stephen Stills
    c. Charles Manson

****

13. Which of the following groups did the Vanilla Fudge not perform with in its 1967 debut at the Village Theatre ?
    a. the Byrds
    b. the Seeds
    c. the Outsiders

****

14. Who wrote the Vogues' 1965 hit *You're the One* ?
    a. Tommy Roe
    b. Petula Clark
    c. Tom Jones

****

15. Who was the Hollies hit *Jennifer Eccles* named after ?
    a. a comic book character
    b. their wives
    c. a female singer

16. In what Francis Ford Coppola movie did the Lovin' Spoonful's *Darling Be Home Soon* appear ?
    a. *Younger Generation*
    b. *What's Up Tiger Lily ?*
    c. *You're a Big Boy Now*

****

17. Who wrote *Dandy,* a 1966 Top 20 hit for Herman's Hermits ?
    a. Herman's Hermits' Peter Noone
    b. John Lennon/Paul McCartney
    c. the Kinks' Ray Davies

****

18. What was Paul Revere & the Raiders' only #1 hit ?
    a. *Good Thing*
    b. *Indian Reservation*
    c. *Kicks*

****

19. What line were the Doors asked to alter or omit when they performed *Light My Fire* on *The Ed Sullivan Show* in 1967 ?
    a. "girl, we couldn't get much higher"
    b. "try to set the night on fire"
    c. "come on baby, light my fire"

****

20. Which rock song contains the oldest lyric ever on a hit single ?
    a. *The Game of Love* / Wayne Fontana & the Mindbenders
    b. *Turn! Turn! Turn!* / Byrds
    c. *The Ten Commandments of Love* / Moonglows

HARDER QUESTIONS: Worth 2 points each — 4 points if
you can answer the question without the three choices !
****

1. What is the only hit song Herman's Hermits ever
   recorded in America ?
   > a. *Mrs. Brown You've Got a Lovely Daughter*
   > b. *I'm Henry VIII I Am*
   > c. *A Must to Avoid*
****

2. Who first gave the Beatles the name the "Beetles" ?
   > a. Brian Epstein
   > b. Stu Sutcliffe
   > c. Paul McCartney
****

3. The 1965 Kingsmen hit *The Jolly Green Giant* was an
   imitation of what 1960 song ?
   > a. *A Little Bitty Tear* / Burl Ives
   > b. *Charlie Brown* / Coasters
   > c. *Big Boy Pete* / Olympics
****

4. Who said the following: "I enjoy performing other
   people's songs. I'm not a musician. When I hear a song
   that I like, I sing it as a part that myself as an actor can
   play — that's basically what I am: an actor but on the
   rock & roll stage."
   > a. Eric Burdon
   > b. Roger Daltry
   > c. Davy Jones
****

5. Which song did John Lennon once call "the best rock
   song ever recorded" ?
   > a. *Whole Lotta Shakin' Going On* / Jerry Lee Lewis
   > b. *Stand By Me* / Ben E. King
   > c. *Roll Over Beethoven* / Chuck Berry

ANSWERS

****

1. c. *The Mighty Quinn*
2. b. David Crosby (of Crosby, Stills & Nash; Hillman's Souther Hillman Furay band was not highly successful commercially)
3. a. *People Got to Be Free* (#1 for 5 weeks...*Groovin'* was #1 for 4 weeks)
4. a. *Over & Over*
5. a. a motorcycle accident in 1966
6. c. Glen Campbell
7. a. *Can't Help Falling In Love*
8. b. *Monday, Monday*
9. b. *Gloria* (recorded originally by his group, Them)
10. a. Neil Diamond
11. c. Paul Revere & the Raiders
12. a. Sonny Bono (others who *did* apply included Paul Williams and Danny Hutton—a founder of Three Dog Night...and, believe it or not, Charles Manson did audition to become a Monkee!)
13. c. the Outsiders
14. b. Petula Clark
15. b. their wives (Allan Clarke's wife's first name & Graham Nash's wife's maiden name)
16. c. *You're a Big Boy Now*
17. c. the Kinks' Ray Davies (Hermits' lead singer Peter Noon recalled it as "perfect for Herman's Hermits" because "it was a song about Dandy—it was a song about me".)
18. b. *Indian Reservation* (#1 for one week in 1971)
19. a. "girl, we couldn't get much higher" (Jim Morrison sang the original line, and the Doors never appeared on *The Ed Sullivan Show* again!)
20. b. *Turn! Turn! Turn!* /Byrds (lyrics are from the book of Ecclesiastes—from the Bible)

****

HARDER QUESTIONS--Answers

1. c. *A Must to Avoid* (which was recorded during the filming of MGM's *Hold On!*)
2. b. Stu Sutcliffe (one of the group's original members)
3. c. *Big Boy Pete* (the Olympics minor hit contained the same beat and bass-voices but had different words—the words, by the way, concern a bar-room confrontation between Big Boy Pete and Bad Man Brown, which ends in a fight in which Bad Man Brown cuts up Big Boy Pete...Sound familiar ? Perhaps Jim Croce and the Kingsmen actually had something in common, which is indeed another interesting piece of trivia!)
4. a. Eric Burdon
5. a. *Whole Lotta Shakin' Going On* / Jerry Lee Lewis

1. Who founded the Reprise record label ?
>   a. Herb Alpert
>   b. Frank Sinatra
>   c. Neil Young

****

2. What stage antic became a Who trademark ?
>   a. setting fire to their equipment
>   b. tossing a large rubber ball into the audience
>   c. smashing their guitars

****

3. What group was being discussed when one member said the following: "There comes a time when you have to draw the line as a man . . . We all play instruments, but we didn't on any of our records up to then. Furthermore, our [record] company doesn't want us to."
>   a. the Byrds
>   b. the Monkees
>   c. Herman's Hermits

****

4. Who was the original fifth Beatle ?
>   a. Billy Fury
>   b. Stu Sutcliffe
>   c. Peter Asher

****

5. What was the Buckinghams' first hit, and only #1 hit ?
>   a. *Kind of a Drag*
>   b. *Mercy, Mercy, Mercy*
>   c. *Don't You Care*

6. Who was the Hollies' 1967 hit *Carrie-Ann* written about ?

      a. actress Ann-Margret

      b. Carrie-Ann Clarke, Allan Clarke's wife

      c. singer Marianne Faithful

****

7. Who was known as the "Godfather of Soul" ?

      a. Otis Redding

      b. Ray Charles

      c. James Brown

****

8. Which of the following people did Bob Dylan consider a major influence in his early career ?

      a. Woody Guthrie

      b. Pete Seger

      c. Dylan Thomas

****

9. Which American band did Beatles manager Brian Epstein also manage ?

      a. the Strawberry Alarm Clock

      b. the Cyrkle

      c. Count Five

****

10. What group, for which Jimi Hendrix was the opening act, is being referred to: "Finally in New York, the yelling for us got so bad during Jimi's set that he . . . threw his guitar down, flipped everyone the bird and walked off the stage."

      a. the Monkees

      b. the Doors

      c. the Beatles

11. What little-known Detroit Wheels song, recorded without Mitch Ryder in the late '60s, was a tribute to a psychedelic drug ?

> a. *Pushin' Up*
> b. *Living in Ecstasy*
> c. *Linda Sue Dixon*

****

12. Who was the writer/producer of Arthur Conley's 1967 hit *Sweet Soul Music* ?

> a. Smokey Robinson
> b. Otis Redding
> c. Lou Rawls

****

13. What inspired Tommy James to name his Top 5 hit *Mony Mony* ?

> a. an X-rated film
> b. his desperate need for money, money
> c. the Mutual of New York building

****

14. Which of the following was the Rolling Stones' first "Top 20" U.S. hit ?

> a. *The Last Time*
> b. *Time Is On My Side*
> c. *19 th Nervous Breakdown*

****

15. On what famous U.S. variety show did the Beatles break into the American music scene ?

> a. *The Ed Sullivan Show*
> b. *Hullabaloo*
> c. *Dick Clark's American Bandstand*

16. Who first recorded and released the hit *Go Now* ?

    a. The Moody Blues

    b. Bessie Banks

    c. Big Mama Thornton

****

17. Who penned three of the four hits sung by Billy J. Kramer & the Dakotas ?

    a. John Lennon and Paul McCartney

    b. Mick Jagger and Keith Richards

    c. Eddie Holland, Lamont Dozier, and Brian Holland

****

18. In what Broadway musical did Davy Jones perform before becoming a Monkee ?

    a. *Jesus Christ Superstar*

    b. *Oliver*

    c. *West Side Story*

****

19. Who did Ringo Starr replace as drummer for the Beatles ?

    a. Stu Sutcliffe

    b. Pete Best

    c. Rory Storm

****

20. On what variety show did the Doors debut their 1969 hit *Touch Me* ?

    a. *The Tonight Show*

    b. *The Ed Sullivan Show*

    c. *The Smothers Brothers Comedy Hour*

HARDER QUESTIONS: Worth 2 points each — 4 points if you can answer the question without the three choices !

****

1. From what group's B-side track did the McCoys derive their name ?

    a. the Beatles
    b. the Four Seasons
    c. the Ventures

****

2. Where did John Lennon and Paul McCartney first meet ?

    a. at a soccer match
    b. at a cafè
    c. at a church picnic

****

3. What song is being referred to in the following by a '60s musicologist: "There has been no song remotely like this one in the . . . history of rock music — strident and bitter, its references blatantly topical."

    a. *Sympathy for the Devil* / Rolling Stones
    b. *My Generation* / Who
    c. *Eve of Destruction* / Barry McGuire

****

4. His father topped the record charts as did he and his sons. Who was this '60s rock star ?

    a. Gary Lewis
    b. Rick Nelson
    c. Donovan

****

5. Who played harmonica on Millie Small's hit *My Boy Lollipop* ?

    a. Rod Stewart
    b. Little Stevie Wonder
    c. Bruce Channel

ANSWERS

****

1. b. Frank Sinatra
2. c. smashing their guitars
3. b. the Monkees (Michael Nesmith's comments)
4. b. Stu Sutcliffe (bass guitarist)
5. a. *Kind of a Drag* (released on the *U.S.A.* label)
6. c. singer Marianne Faithful (slight name-change "to protect the innocent")
7. c. James Brown
8. a. Woody Guthrie
9. b. the Cyrkle (he also gave the group their name)
10. a. the Monkees (comments made by Michael Nesmith; Jimi and his group were soon dropped from the 1967 tour billing)
11. c. *Linda Sue Dixon*
12. b. Otis Redding (also referred to in the song itself)
13. c. the Mutual of New York building (Unable to put the right words to an instrumental track, he got the idea of "Mony" as he looked out his window and saw a sign with those now-famous words. He abbreviated them and turned the letters into gold.)
14. b. *Time Is On My Side* (in November, 1964)
15. a. *The Ed Sullivan Show* (February 9, 1964)
16. a. The Moody Blues (Many have thought that Bessie Banks released the first version of *Go Now*, which was indeed written by her husband, Bertie Banks. But, according to original Moody Blues member Justin Hayward, the song "was only a demo and it came to the Moodies, so the Moodies was the original version to be released". It became the group's first Top 20 hit.)
17. a. John Lennon and Paul McCartney (both of whom wrote *Bad to Me, I'll Keep You Satisfied,* and *From a Window*)
18. b. *Oliver* (he was the Artful Dodger)
19. b. Pete Best
20. c. *The Smothers Brothers Comedy Hour* (with an accompanying orchestral brass section)

****

HARDER QUESTIONS--Answers

1. c. the Ventures (*The McCoy* was the flip-side of *Walk Don't Run*)
2. c. at a church picnic (in 1956)
3. c. *Eve of Destruction* / Barry McGuire (this P.F. Sloan composition is perhaps even more relevant today!)
4. b. Rick Nelson (his father, Ozzie Nelson, topped the charts in 1933; his sons, Gunnar and Matthew, topped the charts in 1990)
5. a. Rod Stewart

1. Under what name did the Animals first record ?

    a. the Wild Cats

    b. the Newcastle Knights

    c. the Alan Price Combo

****

2. Which radio disc jockey was affectionately known as the "Fifth Beatle" ?

    a. Wolfman Jack

    b. Bob "The Beard" Lowrie

    c. Murray the K

****

3. The Young Rascals changed their name to The Rascals right before the release of which Top 20 hit ?

    a. *Groovin'*

    b. *People Got to Be Free*

    c. *A Beautiful Morning*

****

4. Where did the Grateful Dead, along with the Jefferson Airplane, play in 1965 to commemorate opening day for this now–legendary site ?

    a. the Night Owl

    b. Fillmore West

    c. Grumman's Chinese Theatre

****

5. What words in the original version of the Kinks' *Lola* had to be changed ?

    a. "she made me a man"

    b. "girls will be boys and boys will be girls"

    c. "it tastes just like Coca–Cola"

6. Keith Moon died in the same apartment that another famous rocker had died in four years prior. Who was that star ?

     a. Mama Cass Elliot

     b. Brian Jones

     c. Jim Morrison

****

7. Which of the following was <u>not</u> a name used before they were called the Byrds ?

     a. the Beefeaters

     b. the Jet Set

     c. the Mugwumps

****

8. Beatle George Harrison performed a guitar lick on Cream's *Badge.* On what Beatles song did Eric Clapton play lead guitar ?

     a. *While My Guitar Gently Weeps*

     b. *Nowhere Man*

     c. *Here Comes the Sun*

****

9. The Band was the backup for which famous rocker in the '60s ?

     a. Bob Dylan

     b. Neil Diamond

     c. Janis Joplin

****

10. Caesar & Cleo was an earlier name for which performers ?

     a. Simon & Garfunkel

     b. Sonny & Cher

     c. Sam & Dave

11. What profession did Petula Clark initially set out to pursue ?

        a. singing on Broadway

        b. the medical profession

        c. acting

****

12. What was the Grass Roots' highest–charting single ?

        a. *Sooner or Later*

        b. *Midnight Confessions*

        c. *Let's Live for Today*

****

13. What famous rock–idol–to–be appeared on the now–famous *Ed Sullivan Show* which first featured the Beatles in 1964 ?

        a. David Cassidy

        b. Elton John

        c. David Jones

****

14. The Guess Who's first hit, *Shakin' All Over,* was actually released under a former group name. What was it ?

        a. G. Q. & the Silvertones

        b. Chad Allen & the Expressions

        c. Randy & the Reflections

****

15. What was the only song performed by Jimi Hendrix to break into the Top 40 rock charts ?

        a. *Foxy Lady*

        b. *Purple Haze*

        c. *All Along the Watchtower*

16. Before reaching fame as Creedence Clearwater Revival, what were they known as ?

    a. Fantasy

    b. the Golliwogs

    c. Willy & the Poor Boys

****

17. What was the real (birth) name of Ringo Starr ?

    a. Richard Starkey

    b. Harold Masters

    c. Nesbitt McFadden

****

18. Which group's members suggested the name Led Zeppelin ?

    a. the Who

    b. the Yardbirds

    c. Cream

****

19. What song influenced Sonny Bono's writing of *I Got You Babe* ?

    a. *It Ain't Me Babe*

    b. *Be My Baby*

    c. *Don't Worry Baby*

****

20. What is the #1 selling record of all time ?

    a. *Hey Jude* / Beatles

    b. *White Christmas* / Bing Crosby

    c. *Billie Jean* / Michael Jackson

HARDER QUESTIONS: Worth 2 points each — 4 points if you can answer the question without the three choices !
****

1. On what melody is Procol Harum's *A Whiter Shade of Pale* based ?

     a. *Bolero*

     b. *Francesca da Rimini*

     c. *Sleepers Awake*
****

2. Whose guitar work on Nancy Sinatra's 1966 hit *These Boots Are Made for Walking* gave the song a distinctive "boots walking" sound ?

     a. Duane Eddy

     b. Les Paul

     c. John Hartford
****

3. What famous '60s rocker became an early publisher of Bob Seger's songs ?

     a. Del Shannon

     b. Lou Christie

     c. Paul Anka
****

4. Who was the manager for the Sunrays, a Los Angeles surf-band of the mid-'60s ?

     a. Brian Epstein

     b. Murry Wilson

     c. Sonny Bono
****

5. How many Grammy Awards did the Beatles receive for their recordings ?

     a. eight

     b. eleven

     c. twenty-four

ANSWERS

1. c. the Alan Price Combo (Alan Price was keyboardist for the original Animals)
2. c. Murray the K—a top New York deejay. (Bob Lowrie was known as the "Fifth Rascal", and as an aside, Mike "The Mighty Leader" Hamlin was known as the "Fifth Seed". Wolfman Jack was famous for his 1970's *Midnight Special* music-variety show)
3. c. *A Beautiful Morning* (which broke into the Top 10 in May, 1968)
4. b. Fillmore West (in San Francisco—produced by Bill Graham)
5. c. "it tastes just like Coca-Cola" was changed to "it tastes just like cherry cola"
6. a. Mama Cass Elliot (in 1974—Moon died in 1978)
7. c. the Mugwumps
8. a. *While My Guitar Gently Weeps* (from the *White Album*)
9. a. Bob Dylan
10. b. Sonny & Cher
11. c. acting (As Petula Clark recalls, "I'm basically an actress...that's what I wanted to be—I didn't want to be a singer [but] singing just came along.")
12. b. *Midnight Confessions* (#5 in 1969)
13. c. David Jones (later to become lead singer of the Monkees; he appeared as part of the Broadway musical cast of *Oliver*)
14. b. Chad Allen & the Expressions (Chad Allen sang lead vocals on the track)
15. c. *All Along the Watchtower* (which reached #20 in 1968)
16. b. the Golliwogs
17. a. Richard Starkey
18. a. the Who (specifically, members Keith Moon and John Entwistle, who thought that a supergroup with members like Jimmy Page and Steve Winwood would flop like a lead balloon—hence, Led Zeppelin)
19. a. *It Ain't Me Babe* (As Sonny recalls, not only was the "babe" a catchy word, but Dylan's voice also added to the incentive: "This guy sings horribly—I can do what he does...I sing horribly, too!")
20. b. *White Christmas* / Bing Crosby (written by Irving Berlin, first recorded in 1942 for the movie *Holiday Inn,* and featuring the Ken Darby Singers—which, incidentally, re-entered the British Top 20 charts in December, 1977!)

HARDER QUESTIONS--Answers

1. c. *Sleepers Awake* (a cantata by Bach)
2. a. Duane Eddy
3. a. Del Shannon
4. b. Murry Wilson (the Beach Boys' father—spelled Murry, not Murray—who wanted to prove his managing ability by making the band more popular than the Beach Boys themselves—which of course never happened)
5. b. eleven (the first of which was for *A Hard Day's Night*)

1. What inspired Steppenwolf's producer in naming the band ?

> a. a German fairy tale
>
> b. the name of one of Jupiter's moons
>
> c. a novel

****

2. For which group did Three Dog Night leader Danny Hutton audition unsuccessfully before forming his new band ?

> a. the Monkees
>
> b. the Standells
>
> c. the Grass Roots

****

3. From what three '60s bands did Crosby, Stills, Nash & Young evolve ?

> a. Jefferson Airplane/Yardbirds/Zombies
>
> b. Cannet Heat/Spirit/Grass Roots
>
> c. Byrds/Buffalo Springfield/Hollies

****

4. Steveland Morris Hardaway was the real (birth) name for which of the following ?

> a. Steve Miller
>
> b. Stevie Wonder
>
> c. Otis Redding

****

5. What was the name of the Moody Blues' own label, started in 1969 ?

> a. Threshold
>
> b. Deram
>
> c. Virgin

6. What American group did the British Deep Purple emulate ?

    a. Tommy James & the Shondells

    b. The Jimi Hendrix Experience

    c. Vanilla Fudge

****

7. In what now-historic 1965 concert did the Young Rascals play ?

    a. Altamont

    b. the Newport Folk Festival

    c. Shea Stadium

****

8. In which two 1969 films did Steppenwolf songs appear ?

    a. *People* and *The Games*

    b. *Midnight Cowboy* and *Woodstock*

    c. *Candy* and *Easy Rider*

****

9. For what television show in the '70s did Lovin' Spoonful leader John Sebastian sing the theme song ?

    a. *The Jeffersons*

    b. *Welcome Back, Kotter*

    c. *The Love Boat*

****

10. Naomi Cohen was the real (birth) name for which of the following musical performers ?

    a. Mama Cass Elliot

    b. Vicki Lawrence

    c. Dionne Warwick

11. What was the reason for Joe Cocker's on-stage spastic movements ?

    a. It was an uncontrollable reaction to stage fright.

    b. It mimicked Ray Charles' piano-playing style.

    c. It came from an early childhood condition.

****

12. Which classic Led Zeppelin song was never released as a single ?

    a. *D'Yer Mak'er*

    b. *Whole Lotta Love*

    c. *Stairway to Heaven*

****

13. After what famous beer is Creedence Clearwater Revival named ?

    a. Olympia

    b. Hamms

    c. Coors

****

14. Why did Eric Clapton, Jack Bruce, and Ginger Baker call themselves Cream ?

a. They wanted a household word that people used daily.

b. They considered themselves the "cream of the crop."

c. It was a shortened form of an original name, Crushed Dream.

****

15. Which of the following groups was <u>not</u> an offshoot of the Buffalo Springfield ?

    a. the Flying Burrito Brothers

    b. Crosby, Stills, Nash & Young

    c. Poco

16. Perry Miller was the real (birth) name for which of the following ?

> a. Tommy James
> b. Donovan
> c. Jesse Colin Young

****

17. In what two famous music venues did Santana appear in 1968–1969 ?

> a. at Monterey Pop and in San Francisco Park
> b. at Fillmore West and Woodstock Music Festival
> c. at Altamont and the Whiskey A-Go-Go club

****

18. What was the last year in which the Beatles hit *Love Me Do* charted in the British Top 20 ?

> a. 1962
> b. 1972
> c. 1982

****

19. On what famous San Francisco street did the Grateful Dead reside, amid the hippies and the drugs ?

> a. Haight
> b. Ashbury
> c. Market Street

****

20. What never-released 1968 television show featured performances by Eric Clapton, the Who, and John Lennon, along with the Rolling Stones ?

> a. *Sympathy For the Devil*
> b. *Royal Variety Show*
> c. *Rock & Roll Circus*

HARDER QUESTIONS: Worth 2 points each — 4 points if you can answer the question without the three choices !

****

1. What was the Monkees last U.S. Top 20 single ?
   - a. *Valleri*
   - b. *D.W. Washburn*
   - c. *Words*

****

2. What have been named Lennon, McCartney, Harrison and Starr to ensure immortality for the Beatles ?
   - a. four British cars
   - b. the trophies given out at the New Musical Express annual awards
   - c. four asteroids

****

3. On what variety show did Iron Butterfly make their debut network performance ?
   - a. *The Smothers Brothers Comedy Hour*
   - b. *The Ed Sullivan Show*
   - c. *The Red Skelton Show*

****

4. What was the motive behind the Mamas & the Papas' John Phillips writing *I Saw Her Again (Last Night)* ?
   - a. revenge
   - b. it was a subtle marriage proposal
   - c. it was a tribute to the group's devoted fans

****

5. What inspired the Animal's *San Franciscan Nights* ?
   - a. a night at the Fillmore West
   - b. a television documentary on the city
   - c. a dream that Eric Burdon had one night

ANSWERS

****

1. c. a novel by Herman Hesse
2. a. the Monkees
3. c. Byrds/Buffalo Springfield/Hollies (Byrds: David Crosby; Buffalo Springfield: Stephen Stills and Neil Young; Hollies: Graham Nash)
4. b. Stevie Wonder (birth name also reported as: B. Steveland Judkins)
5. a. Threshold
6. c. Vanilla Fudge (whose first Top 40 hit charted only a month before their own first hit, *Hush*)
7. c. Shea Stadium (as an opening act for the Beatles' New York sell-out)
8. c. *Candy* and *Easy Rider* (each of which also included songs by the Byrds)
9. b. *Welcome Back, Kotter*
10. a. Mama Cass Elliot (of the Mamas & the Papas)
11. b. It mimicked Ray Charles' piano-playing style. (Joe Cocker was <u>not</u> spastic)
12. c. *Stairway to Heaven* (from *Led Zeppelin 4*)
13. a. Olympia (which came from Clearwater, Washington)
14. b. They considered themselves the "cream of the crop" of British blues players.
15. a. the Flying Burrito Brothers
16. c. Jesse Colin Young (Youngbloods leader)
17. b. Fillmore West (1968) and Woodstock (1969)
18. c. 1982 (Along with the Animals' *House of the Rising Sun,* The Beatles' *Love Me Do* returned briefly into the Top 20 British Singles charts in October, 1982!)
19. b. Ashbury (in a communal setting at 710 Ashbury Street)
20. c. *Rock & Roll Circus* (the performances have since been shown on VH-1 on rare occasions)

****

HARDER QUESTIONS--Answers

1. b. *D.W. Washburn*
2. c. four asteroids (discovered in 1983 and 1984 and named for the Beatles)
3. c. *The Red Skelton Show* (in 1968, during which time they played the *Iron Butterfly Theme* song)
4. a. revenge (John Phillips wrote the song, which lead singer Denny Doherty would then have to sing on stage, exposing the affair Denny was having with John's wife, Michelle Phillips.)
5. a. a night at the Fillmore West (Eric Burdon recalls that on one unusually hot evening while they were performing, people spilled out into the streets, enjoying the Haight-Ashbury style love-in feeling—and, as he put it, he wanted to "capture the feeling" in a song.)

1. What prompted the Byrds to write and sing *Eight Miles High* ?
> a. a drug experience aboard a plane
> b. a recent trip to England
> c. the Beatles song *Eight Days a Week*

****

2. What top British band of the late '60s was Rod Stewart <u>not</u> a member of ?
> a. the Hollies
> b. the Faces
> c. the Jeff Beck Group

****

3. What is the origin of the name Three Dog Night ?
> a. It's a takeoff on the Beatles' movie *A Hard Day's Night.*
> b. It's the name of their first gig, a coffeehouse nightclub.
> c. It's an Australian term for a very cold night.

****

4. What did the Grateful Dead call themselves before turning to their immortal Dead moniker ?
> a. Jerry & the Cycles
> b. the Bottom Step
> c. the Warlocks

****

5. At which Rolling Stones concert did the *Hell's Angels* serve as security ?
> a. Hyde Park
> b. Asbury Park
> c. Altamont

6. What was the name of the newly-formed group after the Yardbirds broke up, prior to the renaming of the new group as Led Zeppelin ?

        a. Heavy Metal Thunder

        b. the New Yardbirds

        c. the Bluesbreakers

****

7. What was the name of Joe Cocker's forty-three-piece band ?

        a. the Compass Pointers

        b. Mad Dogs & Englishmen

        c. the British Connection

****

8. What did Jim Morrison die from ?

        a. a heart attack

        b. a drug overdose

        c. suicide

****

9. With regard to Gary Puckett & the Union Gap, in which state is Union Gap ?

        a. New York

        b. Pennsylvania

        c. Washington

****

10. What was Vanilla Fudge's only Top 10 hit ?

        a. *You Keep Me Hangin' On*

        b. *Eleanor Rigby*

        c. *Take Me For a Little While*

11. What group did Outsiders' lead singer Sonny Geraci form in the early '70s ?
   a. Atlanta Rhythm Section
   b. Climax
   c. Orleans

****

12. What was Santana's only song from the '60s <u>not</u> sung in English that broke into the Top 20 charts ?
   a. *Oye Como Va*
   b. *Jingo*
   c. *Black Magic Woman*

****

13. Who wrote Badfinger's first hit, *Come & Get It* ?
   a. Tommy James
   b. Paul McCartney
   c. Dave Clark

****

14. Anna May Bullock was the real (birth) name for which of the following music superstars ?
   a. Tina Turner
   b. Janis Joplin
   c. Aretha Franklin

****

15. Which song was recorded by the Moody Blues in 1968, then released as a single in 1972 and re-released in 1978 ?
   a. *Your Wildest Dreams*
   b. *The Story in Your Eyes*
   c. *Nights in White Satin*

16. What famous 1969 music festival did Sly & the Family Stone <u>not</u> appear in ?

      a. Altamont

      b. the Newport Jazz Festival

      c. Woodstock

****

17. Where did Who leader Pete Townshend lose part of his hearing due to a pyro-technics performance malfunction ?

      a. at the Fillmore West

      b. at Woodstock

      c. during a television appearance

****

18. Who wrote Three Dog Night's biggest hit, *Joy to the World* ?

      a. Randy Newman

      b. Harry Nilsson

      c. Hoyt Axton

****

19. What experience affected the Grateful Dead's early music and won the group a different following ?

      a. watching a Jimi Hendrix performance

      b. experimentation with LSD

      c. a religious conversion

****

20. What well-known British group backed Donovan in his *Barabajagal* album ?

      a. the Jeff Beck Group

      b. the Moody Blues

      c. the Hollies

****

1. Reportedly, who was Carly Simon's *You're So Vain*
   written about ?

   a. Mick Jagger

   b. James Taylor

   c. Warren Beatty

****

2. With what '60s band did Steely Dan leader Donald Fagen
   help out as a backup keyboardist and vocalist ?

   a. the Turtles

   b. Iron Butterfly

   c. Jay & the Americans

****

3. What group did singer Greg Lake leave just prior to
   forming Emerson, Lake & Palmer ?

   a. King Crimson

   b. the Nice

   c. the Small Faces

****

4. What group had a three-single deal with their record
   company, but when the first two records failed to chart,
   the company told them that they'd have to pay for the
   studio time themselves for the third single ?

   a. the Buckinghams

   b. the Left Banke

   c. the Kinks

****

5. Who said the following: "You like people ? I hate
   'em . . . screw 'em . . . I don't need 'em . . ."

   a. Mick Jagger

   b. Jim Morrison

   c. John Lennon

ANSWERS

1. b. a recent trip to England (The song was a reflection of the "rain grey town" and of the street signs that don't really guide you, a land that is stranger than it is known. Needless to say, the Byrds' arrival was not well-received by the Britishers either, most of whom unjustly felt the American group a threat to the British Merseybeat dominance...Several venues were cancelled due to low ticket-sales, and the song itself failed to perform well in the U.S.A.—due to another false-association that it was drug-related.)

2. a. the Hollies

3. c. It's an Australian term for a very cold night (in which one needs three dogs to supply the needed warmth while outdoors).

4. c. the Warlocks

5. c. Altamont (a gun-waving fan was killed during the 1969 California concert)

6. b. the New Yardbirds

7. b. Mad Dogs & Englishmen

8. a. a heart attack (in Paris, 1971)

9. c. Washington (near where leader Gary Puckett grew up)

10. a. *You Keep Me Hangin' On* (#6 in 1968)

11. b. Climax (who charted with *Precious & Few* in 1972)

12. a. *Oye Como Va*

13. b. Paul McCartney (it appeared in the film *The Magic Christian*)

14. a. Tina Turner

15. c. *Nights in White Satin*

16. a. Altamont

17. c. during a television appearance (During the group's 1967 appearance on the *Smothers Brothers Comedy Hour,* drummer Keith Moon secretly planted explosives in the drum set, planning for a loud finish to their appearance. However, the explosion was so great that it blew out one of Townshend's eardrums, resulting in permanent restricted hearing. In addition, in the pandemonium a guitar was also thrown in the air, hitting Townshend in the head and leaving him stunned as he exited the stage. The performance was memorable, but for many of the wrong reasons.)

18. c. Hoyt Axton (country singer and writer)

19. b. experimentation with LSD

20. a. the Jeff Beck Group

HARDER QUESTIONS--Answers

1. c. Warren Beatty (Mick Jagger sang on the record but was not the target of the lyrics)

2. c. Jay & the Americans

3. a. King Crimson

4. c. the Kinks (Ray Davies adds: "That was really cruel because [Pye Records] knew we were broke.")

5. b. Jim Morrison

1. Which of the following groups did Eric Clapton
   not form ?
   > a. the Yardbirds
   > b. Cream
   > c. Blind Faith

****

2. What is the only '60s group to equal the Beatles
   record of 8 million-selling hits in one year ?
   > a. the Four Seasons
   > b. Creedence Clearwater Revival
   > c. the Beach Boys

****

3. Marie Lawrie was the real (birth) name for which of the
   following ?
   > a. Lulu
   > b. Anne Murray
   > c. Laurie London

****

4. In which historic music festival did Joe Cocker appear
   and then reprise ?
   > a. Newport Folk Festival
   > b. Monterey
   > c. Woodstock

****

5. In which Steppenwolf song were the now-legendary
   words "heavy metal" originally found ?
   > a. *Sookie Sookie*
   > b. *Born to Be Wild*
   > c. *Magic Carpet Ride*

6. What was the Grass Roots' first charted single ?
   a. *Where Were You When I Needed You*
   b. *Let's Live For Today*
   c. *Midnight Confessions*

****

7. How did Yardbirds lead singer Keith Relf die ?
   a. in a private plane crash
   b. from pneumonia
   c. he was shot during a riot

****

8. On what TV show did Led Zeppelin make its U.S. debut ?
   a. *The Midnight Special*
   b. *The Sonny & Cher Show*
   c. *Don Kirschner's Rock Concert*

****

9. Who was Crosby, Stills & Nash's 1969 hit *Suite Judy Blue Eyes* written about ?
   a. '50s movie icon Judy Holliday
   b. singer/songwriter Judy Collins
   c. a character in a Cary Grant movie

****

10. What legendary singer sang lead for the '60s group Big Brother & the Holding Company ?
    a. Linda Ronstadt
    b. Janis Joplin
    c. Mama Cass Elliot

11. What two other group names stemmed from the
    original Jefferson Airplane ?
    a. the Jets and Cloudburst
    b. Airplane and Concorde
    c. Jefferson Starship and Starship

****

12. With what group did leader Eric Burdon record after
    leaving the Animals ?
    a. Santana
    b. War
    c. Foghat

****

13. Which 1969 hit generally popularized the phrase
    "different strokes for different folks" ?
    a. *Everyday People* / Sly & the Family Stone
    b. *It's Your Thing* / Isley Brothers
    c. *Sugar Sugar* / Archies

****

14. Which former member of the Zombies scored a Top 10
    solo hit in 1972 ?
    a. Colin Bluntstone
    b. Chris White
    c. Rod Argent

****

15. At what now infamous concert did the Grateful Dead
    perform in 1969 ?
    a. Altamont
    b. the Monterey Pop Festival
    c. Concert at Golden Gate Park

16. What was the Beatles' last official U.S. single ?
    a. *The Long & Winding Road*
    b. *Let It Be*
    c. *Come Together*

****

17. What is the actual spelling of the group that made the 1969 hit *More Today Than Yesterday* ?
    a. Spiral Staircase
    b. Spiral Starecase
    c. Spyryl Staircase

****

18. Who was the first artist released on the Beatles' Apple label ?
    a. the Beatles
    b. Billy Preston
    c Mary Hopkin

****

19. What was the name of the 1979 television documentary film on the Who ?
    a. *The Kids are Alright*
    b. *Tommy*
    c. *Quadrophenia*

****

20. Which 1967 music festival in San Francisco featured the Grateful Dead and the Jefferson Airplane, attracting 20,000 people ?
    a. the Monterey Pop Festival
    b. the Golden Gate Public Benefit concert
    c. the Human Be-In

HARDER QUESTIONS: Worth 2 points each — 4 points if you can answer the question without the three choices !
****

1. What was New York's Fillmore East music venue formerly known as ?
   a. Greenwich Auditorium
   b. Village Threatre
   c. Central Park Pavillion
****

2. What Top 5 hit was sung by a member of Survivor in an earlier band in 1970 ?
   a. *All Right Now* / Free
   b. *Ride Captain Ride* / Blues Image
   c. *Vehicle* / Ides of March
****

3. In what year did Petula Clark first break into the Top 20 Singles chart ?
   a. 1954
   b. 1961
   c. 1965
****

4. Cubby O'Brien, of Mousketeer fame, became the drummer for which of the following groups ?
   a. the Carpenters
   b. Every Mother's Son
   c. the Flying Machine
****

5. Who said the following at Woodstock:
   "You can leave if you want to — I'm just jammin'" ?
   a. Pete Townshend
   b. Jimi Hendrix
   c. Bob Marley

ANSWERS

****

1. a. the Yardbirds
2. b. Creedence Clearwater Revival (in 1969)
3. a. Lulu
4. c. Woodstock/Woodstock + 25
5. b. *Born to Be Wild*
6. a. *Where Were You When I Needed You* (a 1966 track that had also been recorded by Herman's Hermits—though never released as a single—and the Turtles)
7. b. from pneumonia (in 1976...another report says he was electrocuted at home while playing his guitar...however, his lifelong frail health makes the former reason seem more credible)
8. c. *Don Kirschner's Rock Concert* (in which they played *Black Dog*)
9. b. singer/songwriter Judy Collins
10. b. Janis Joplin (in the Top 20 hit *Piece of My Heart*)
11. c. Jefferson Starship and Starship
12. b. War
13. a. *Everyday People* / Sly & the Family Stone (By the way, Sylvester Stone, leader of the group, had been a San Francisco deejay before making a splash on the music scene.)
14. c. Rod Argent (the song was *Hold Your Head Up*)
15. a. Altamont (where a belligerent fan was killed during the Stones' performance)
16. a. *The Long & Winding Road* (released in June, 1970)
17. b. Spiral Starecase (it was intentionally misspelled . . . in our Rock Series, we've included the visually-pleasing spelling rather than the actual spelling)
18. c. Mary Hopkin (the Beatles, by the way, were still contracted to Capitol Records)
19. a. *The Kids are Alright*
20. c. the Human Be-In (the first of several to come)

****

HARDER QUESTIONS—Answers

1. b. Village Threatre
2. c. *Vehicle* / Ides of March (featuring Survivor keyboardist Jim Peterik as lead singer)
3. a. 1954 (*The Little Shoemaker,* a French song, broke into the British Top 20 Singles chart in June, 1954, and stayed in the top 20 for three months! Five more Petula Clark songs charted in the British Top 20 Singles chart in the 1950's, then four more in the early 1960's, before she finally cracked into the U.S. Charts with her smash hit *Downtown* in January, 1965.)
4. a. the Carpenters
5. b. Jimi Hendrix

1. What was Aerosmith's first single to break into the Top 40 ?
   - a. *Last Child*
   - b. *Sweet Emotion*
   - c. *Dream On*

****

2. Many likened the voice of America's lead singer Dewey Bunnel in *A Horse With No Name* to that of another 1972 rocker. Who was he ?
   - a. James Taylor
   - b. Neil Young
   - c. Don McLean

****

3. Which country did Bachman-Turner Overdrive come from ?
   - a. Canada
   - b. England
   - c. the U.S.

****

4. What was the Grateful Dead's only Top 20 song ?
   - a. *Touch of Grey*
   - b. *Truckin'*
   - c. *Casey Jones*

****

5. For whom was Elton John's *Candle in the Wind* an ode ?
   - a. Jayne Mansfield
   - b. Natalie Wood
   - c. Marilyn Monroe

6. What was the name of David Bowie's original backup band ?

    a. the Lower Third

    b. the Girls

    c. the Mothers of Invention

****

7. What was the name of the album in which John Lennon and Yoko Ono posed nude for the cover ?

    a. *Some Time In New York City*

    b. *Live Peace in Toronto*

    c. *Two Virgins*

****

8. What Boston single topped the U.S. Charts for two weeks ?

    a. *Amanda*

    b. *Don't Look Back*

    c. *More Than a Feeling*

****

9. Which double-album set, released in 1976, went on to sell over 10 million copies worldwide ?

    a. *Frampton Comes Alive* / Peter Frampton

    b. *The Wall* / Pink Floyd

    c. *Saturday Night Fever* Soundtrack

****

10. In which country was Kiss leader Gene Simmons born ?

    a. the U.S.

    b. Russia

    c. Israel

11. What Canadian transportation company inspired the group name, Grand Funk Railroad ?
      a. the Grand Trunk Railroad
      b. the Grand Junk Railroad
      c. the Graham Funk Trail-load

****

12. Which flaming concert provided the spark for Deep Purple's 1973 hit *Smoke on the Water* ?
      a. the Who at the Monterey Pop Festival
      b. Frank Zappa & the Mothers of Invention at Montreaux
      c. the Rolling Stones at Altamount

****

13. What was Edgar Winter Group's only #1 hit ?
      a. *Easy Street*
      b. *Frankenstein*
      c. *Free Ride*

****

14. Who produced Badfinger's two last hits, *Day After Day* and *Baby Blue* ?
      a. Eric Carmen; David Bowie
      b. George Harrison; Todd Rundgren
      c. James Taylor; Eric Clapton

****

15. For what word is the name Devo a shortened form ?
      a. "devour"
      b. "redevelopment"
      c. "de-evolution"

16. From what did Bad Company select their name ?
>   a. a song from the 1890s
>   b. a 1972 movie
>   c. a brand of jeans

****

17. In what country were the Van Halen brothers born ?
>   a. Holland
>   b. France
>   c. the U.S.

****

18. Why didn't David Bowie sing under his birth name David Jones ?
>   a. He didn't like his initials: DJ.
>   b. There already was a Davy Jones.
>   c. A Buddhist guru suggested the new name for spiritual reasons.

****

19. Which famous '70s guitarist produced and later played for the Edgar Winter Group ?
>   a. Rick Derringer
>   b. Stevie Winwood
>   c. Randy Bachman

****

20. What professional sport did Rod Stewart seriously pursue, though his talents in music proved greater ?
>   a. golf
>   b. tennis
>   c. soccer

HARDER QUESTIONS: Worth 2 points each — 4 points if you can answer the question without the three choices !

****

1. How did Pink Floyd get their name ?

   a. from the *Pink Panther* cartoon

   b. from the names of two blues singers

   c. from the '60s album *Music From Big Pink,* by the Band

****

2. In which 1970 music festival did the Allman Brothers Band play alongside Jimi Hendrix, among others ?

   a. the Fillmore East

   b. Woodstock

   c. the Atlanta International Pop Festival

****

3. How did the band get the name Pretenders ?

   a. from the '50s hit *The Great Pretender*

   b. from rock fans' doubtful reactions as to whether the group was really singing their songs

   c. by picking a word at random from the dictionary

****

4. With what famous blues band did three of the original members of Fleetwood Mac play ?

   a. the Blues Project

   b. the Blues Magoos

   c. John Mayall's Bluesbreakers

****

5. What movie is said to have been the inspiration for Tom Petty's future musical interests ?

   a. *Rebel Without a Cause*

   b. *Follow That Dream*

   c. *2001: A Space Odyssey*

ANSWERS

1. b. *Sweet Emotion* (in 1975)
2. b. Neil Young, whose *Heart of Gold* had also just climbed to #1 on the music charts. Some people actually thought Neil Young had sung the America track under an alias.
3. a. Canada
4. a. *Touch of Grey* (not in the '60s, or even in the '70s . . . it happened in 1987!)
5. c. Marilyn Monroe
6. a. the Lower Third
7. c. *Two Virgins*
8. a. *Amanda*
9. a. *Frampton Comes Alive* / Peter Frampton
10. c. Israel
11. a. the Grand Trunk Railroad
12. b. Frank Zappa & the Mothers of Invention at Montreaux (While performing at the Montreaux Casino in Switzerland, a fire erupted, consuming the building as well as $50,000 of the band's music equipment.)
13. b. *Frankenstein,* an instrumental whose title came from the extensive editing and reconstruction done to the originally recorded version. It turned into a monster!
14. b. George Harrison (*Day After Day*); Todd Rundgren (*Baby Blue*)
15. c. "de-evolution" (the band's commentary on the status of mankind)
16. b. a 1972 movie starring Jeff Bridges
17. a. Holland
18. b. There already was a Davy Jones (with the Monkees).
19. a. Rick Derringer, of *Rock & Roll, Hoochie Koo* fame
20. c. soccer

HARDER QUESTIONS--Answers

1. b. from the names of two blues singers: Pink Anderson and Floyd Council
2. c. the Atlanta International Pop Festival
3. a. from the '50s hit *The Great Pretender*
4. c. John Mayall's Bluesbreakers
5. b. *Follow That Dream* (starring Elvis Presley and filmed near Tom Petty's home while he was a youngster)

1. *Black Water* was the Doobie Brothers' first #1 hit. What was their second and final #1 single ?
   - a. *What a Fool Believes*
   - b. *Takin' It to the Streets*
   - c. *Real Love*

****

2. Daryl Hall & John Oates became the most successful duo in the history of rock & roll, with more #1 hits than any other rock two-some. Which duo did they surpass for this honor ?
   - a. the Everly Brothers
   - b. Sonny & Cher
   - c. Simon & Garfunkel

****

3. What unusual physical characteristic has made Edgar Winter unique in rock & roll ?
   - a. He is 6'11", the tallest rocker.
   - b. He has six fingers on one hand.
   - c. He is albino.

****

4. What on-stage eccentricity made Jethro Tull flutist Ian Anderson unique to the music world ?
   - a. He would shake uncontrollably during his performance.
   - b. He would often play while standing on one foot.
   - c. He would play the flute through his nose.

****

5. What was Elton John's birth name ?
   - a. Paul Madrid
   - b. Ian Brooks
   - c. Reginald Dwight

6. How did Lynyrd Skynyrd get their name ?
   a. It was an abbreviated name for two bands, Sky Lion and the Byrds.
   b. They named themselves after a gym teacher.
   c. A local deejay suggested it during an early performance.

****

7. How did Jim Croce die ?
   a. in a hang–gliding accident
   b. in a plane crash
   c. from a self–inflicted gunshot

****

8. Who was Elton John's *Empty Garden* written about ?
   a. Marilyn Monroe
   b. John F. Kennedy
   c. John Lennon

****

9. Which '60s American group had a lasting influence on the Eagles, including their name selection as well as their musical style ?
   a. the Turtles
   b. the Byrds
   c. Jefferson Airplane

****

10. What was the first Top 5 hit recorded by Paul McCartney & Wings ?
    a. *Live & Let Die*
    b. *Band on the Run*
    c. *My Love*

11. From what renowned band leader did Steve Miller receive his first guitar lesson ?
    a. Glenn Miller
    b. Mitch Miller
    c. Les Paul

****

12. In what year did Pink Floyd first begin appearing as regulars in London nightclubs ?
    a. 1966
    b. 1970
    c. 1973

****

13. From which group did members of Bad Company not evolve ?
    a. the Guess Who
    b. King Crimson
    c. Free

****

14. What separated David Bowie from other male performers in his '70s concerts ?
    a. He sang in a high falsetto voice.
    b. He had no musical backup band.
    c. He often wore dresses.

****

15. 10cc was named by British music-industry giant Jonathan King. Which of the following groups did he also name ?
    a. Genesis
    b. Thompson Twins
    c. Depeche Mode

16. With what is the name Doobie Brothers associated ?
    a. a joint
    b. the bee on the *Romper Room* children's television show
    c. the cartoon character Scooby Doo

****

17. How did Steely Dan leaders Donald Fagen and Walter Becker first become members of the band ?
    a. by auditioning in a music talent show
    b. from an encounter with other members during a high school football game
    c. through an ad

****

18. Before shortening his group name to Frampton, what was the band called ?
    a. Peter & the Frampton Four
    b. Frampton's Camel
    c. Pframpton Pfrog

****

19. What '60s group did Bachman–Turner Overdrive evolve from ?
    a. the Kingsmen
    b. the Grass Roots
    c. the Guess Who

****

20. Which Aerosmith song was redone as a rap hit ten years later ?
    a. *Walk This Way*
    b. *Dude (Looks Like a Lady)*
    c. *Angel*

HARDER QUESTIONS: Worth 2 points each — 4 points if you can answer the question without the three choices !

****

1. With what top '60s British band did 10cc singer-guitarist Eric Stewart play ?

 a. Manfred Mann

 b. Gerry & the Pacemakers

 c. Wayne Fontana & the Mindbenders

****

2. How did Phil Collins join Genesis as drummer in 1970 ?

 a. He met them at a party.

 b. He responded to a music magazine ad.

 c. He dated the guitarist's sister.

****

3. While in high school, Steve Miller formed his first band, the Marksmen Combo, which included another future star who, in fact, learned the guitar from Steve Miller. Who was this friend ?

 a. Eddie Van Halen

 b. Richie Sambora

 c. Boz Scaggs

****

4. What famous '60s musician played saxophone in Foreigner's *Urgent* ?

 a. Junior Walker

 b. Gary U.S. Bonds

 c. Stan Getz

****

5. ZZ Top has long been a touring sensation. To ensure their future success, where did the band make an advance booking reservation in 1987 to go to ?

 a. the Grammy Awards ceremonies in the year 2020

 b. Woodstock + 50

 c. the moon

ANSWERS

1. a. *What a Fool Believes* (#1 for one week in 1979)
2. a. the Everly Brothers
3. c. He is albino (as is his brother Johnny).
4. b. He would often play while standing on one foot.
5. c. Reginald Dwight
6. b. They named themselves after a gym teacher who didn't like long-haired students. Leonard Skinner actually introduced the band at a local concert years later, which goes to show that rock & roll leaves no hard feelings!
7. b. in a plane crash (in 1973)
8. c. John Lennon, as a tribute
9. b. the Byrds
10. a. *Live & Let Die*
11. c. Les Paul
12. a. 1966
13. a. the Guess Who
14. c. He often wore dresses.
15. a. Genesis (Record producer Jonathan King first gained international fame in 1965 when he wrote and sang *Everyone's Gone to the Moon.*)
16. a. a joint (At the time the name was suggested, the band didn't know of the drug context.)
17. c. It was through an ad in the *Village Voice,* placed there by guitarist Denny Dias, seeking jazz-oriented rockers. Their original drummer was Chevy Chase, who changed professions and made his claim to fame in comedy!
18. b. Frampton's Camel
19. c. the Guess Who (Randy Bachman was the group's lead guitarist)
20. a. *Walk This Way* (re-popular ized in 1986 with the aid of Run-D.M.C.)

HARDER QUESTIONS—Answers

1. c. Wayne Fontana & the Mindbenders (10cc co-leader Graham Gouldman also joined the group after Fontana had left—they were then known simply as the Mindbenders.)
2. b. He responded to a music magazine ad (in *Melody Maker*) seeking a drummer for the band.
3. c. Boz Scaggs
4. a. Junior Walker (formerly of *Shotgun* fame)
5. c. On October 10, 1987, ZZ Top announced that they'd made an advance-booking for the first passenger flight to the moon.

1. What was Billy Idol's only #1 hit in the U.S. ?
>   a. *Mony Mony*
>   b. *Rebel Yell*
>   c. *Eyes Without a Face*

****

2. Why did Chicago shorten their name from Chicago Transit Authority ?
>   a. It wouldn't fit on their album cover.
>   b. It sounded too much like a government agency.
>   c. They were threatened with a lawsuit.

****

3. In what movie did Aerosmith appear, portraying villains ?
>   a. *Jesus Christ Superstar*
>   b. *Sgt. Pepper's Lonely Hearts Club Band*
>   c. *Tommy*

****

4. What did the Edgar Winter Group originally call themselves ?
>   a. White Trash
>   b. Pimentosa Nervosa
>   c. the Blues Experiment

****

5. What was the actual incident that later inspired Elton John's *Someone Saved My Life Tonight* ?
>   a. a reunion between Elton John and Bernie Taupin
>   b. the winning of three Grammy awards
>   c. a suicide attempt by Elton John

6. What album featured the Lynyrd Skynyrd band in flames, as if presaging their fateful plane crash ?

     a. *Street Survivors*

     b. *One More for the Road*

     c. *Free at Last*

****

7. What was Fleetwood Mac's only #1 U.S. hit ?

     a. *Dreams*

     b. *Go Your Own Way*

     c. *Hold Me*

****

8. After whom was the band Jethro Tull named ?

     a. a lesser-known '50s actor

     b. an 18th-century agriculturist

     c. the hero in a 19th-century novel

****

9. Who produced Grand Funk's first #1 hit, *We're An American Band* ?

     a. Bruce Springsteen

     b. Todd Rundgren

     c. Alice Cooper

****

10. Which famous '70s rocker began singing at age fifteen for the McCoys ?

     a. Ted Nugent

     b. Rod Argent

     c. Rick Derringer

11. In which country did Cheap Trick's 1978 concert sell out within two hours ?
    a. England
    b. Japan
    c. Australia

****

12. Who was the inspiration for the name "ZZ Top" ?
    a. Texas blues singer Z.Z. Hill
    b. the manager of a professional football team
    c. rock star Iggy Pop

****

13. In *Sweet Home Alabama,* who did Lynyrd Skynyrd lambaste as being no friend to the South ?
    a. Richard Nixon
    b. Neil Young
    c. George Wallace

****

14. From what '60s rock band did two members and the manager of Atlanta Rhythm Section emanate ?
    a. the Turtles
    b. Blood, Sweat & Tears
    c. Classics IV

****

15. Who played piano on the Hollies' hit *He Ain't Heavy, He's My Brother* ?
    a. Billy Joel
    b. Neil Sedaka
    c. Elton John

16. Who was Elton John's *Daniel* originally written about ?

    a. a Viet Nam veteran

    b. Elton John's drummer, Nigel Olsson

    c. Danny Thomas

****

17. In which album did Kiss first appear without the now-famous Kiss makeup ?

    a. *Kiss*

    b. *Kiss Unmasked*

    c. *Lick It Up*

****

18. How did Duane Allman die ?

    a. he was lost in a hiking expedition

    b. in a motorcycle accident

    c. in an avalanche

****

19. What supergroup did Carl Palmer help form soon after leaving Emerson, Lake & Palmer ?

    a. Styx

    b. Asia

    c. Supertramp

****

20. What was Alice Cooper's birth name ?

    a. Vincent Furnier

    b. Reginald Dwight

    c. Arnold Wiggins

HARDER QUESTIONS: Worth 2 points each — 4 points if you can answer the question without the three choices !
****

1. What underground psychedelic '60s band did ZZ Top leader Billy Gibbons form ?
   - a. Moby Grape
   - b. the Moving Sidewalks
   - c. Southwest F.O.B.

****

2. Which organization selected Kansas as the first group to represent them as its Deputy Ambassadors of Goodwill ?
   - a. UNICEF
   - b. the Boy Scouts of America
   - c. the Benevolent Protective Order of Elks

****

3. Which singer/songwriter said the following:
   "I write the tunes first, then the lyrics, which are dictated by the mood of the music".
   - a. Bob Dylan
   - b. Paul McCartney
   - c. Billy Joel

****

4. For which television series theme song did Toto member David Paich and his father win an Emmy ?
   - a. *Welcome Back, Kotter*
   - b. *Hill Street Blues*
   - c. *Ironside*

****

5. What group was Jackson Browne an original member of ?
   - a. Poco
   - b. Nitty Gritty Dirt Band
   - c. Spiral Staircase

ANSWERS

1. a. *Mony Mony* (a remake of Tommy James & the Shondells' 1968 hit)
2. c. They were threatened with a lawsuit (from the Chicago Transit Authority and Chicago mayor Richard Daley).
3. b. *Sgt. Pepper's Lonely Hearts Club Band*
4. a. White Trash
5. c. A suicide attempt by Elton John, brought on by second thoughts and ensuing depression regarding a forthcoming marriage. The marriage plans were terminated, the song became a testimonial and a hit, and Elton John lives on.
6. a. *Street Survivors* (the cover of which was changed shortly after the fatal incident)
7. a. *Dreams* (#1 for one week in 1977)
8. b. an 18th-century agriculturist who invented the seed drill
9. b. Todd Rundgren
10. c. Rick Derringer (born Rick Zehringer)
11. b. Japan
12. a. Texas blues singer Z.Z. Hill
13. b. Neil Young (to whom they said—in response to Young's attack on the Southern Man—that the "Southern man don't need him around anyhow")
14. c. Classics IV
15. c. Elton John
16. a. A Viet Nam veteran. Writer Bernie Taupin was inspired by an article in *Newsweek* and wrote a tribute to the man it described as fleeing from the lingering memories of the war.
17. c. *Lick It Up*
18. b. in a motorcycle accident (in 1971)
19. b. Asia
20. a. Vincent Damon Furnier

HARDER QUESTIONS--Answers

1. b. the Moving Sidewalks, who opened for the Jimi Hendrix Experience in a 1968 concert
2. a. UNICEF (in 1978)
3. c. Billy Joel
4. c. *Ironside*
5. b. Nitty Gritty Dirt Band

1. The T-Bones, the group which performed the Alka-Seltzer song *No Matter What Shape (Your Stomach's In)*, later became which popular group ?
        a. Atlanta Rhythm Section
        b. Hamilton, Joe Frank & Reynolds
        c. 10cc

****

2. What unique rock and roll idea did each of the four members of Kiss participate in during 1978 ?
a. Each hosted their own rock-radio talk show in different cities.
b. Each sponsored a different commercial product on TV.
c. Each released a solo album.

****

3. Which song did Jackson Browne co-write with Glenn Frey, later to become the Eagles' first Top 20 hit ?
        a. *Take it Easy*
        b. *Witchy Woman*
        c. *Lyin' Eyes*

****

4. For which of the following did Todd Rundgren <u>not</u> produce an album ?
        a. Grand Funk Railroad
        b. Aerosmith
        c. Badfinger

****

5. What heavy-rock garage band did Ted Nugent form in the late '60s ?
        a. the Thirteenth Floor Elevators
        b. the Shadows of Knight
        c. the Amboy Dukes

6. *Another Brick in the Wall (Part II)* was Pink Floyd's biggest hit, hitting #1 for four weeks. What was their only other Top 40 hit ?
>   a. *Money*
>   b. *Echoes*
>   c. *Run Like Hell*

****

7. In what year did the rock band Styx form ?
>   a. 1964
>   b. 1970
>   c. 1974

****

8. *Changes* was David Bowie's first U.S. RCA release. What was his first #1 RCA hit ?
>   a. *Space Oddity*
>   b. *Fame*
>   c. *Young Americans*

****

9. What name did Alice Cooper use for his band before noticing that it was already the name of a band ?
>   a. the Kiss
>   b. the G.T.O.'s
>   c. the Nazz

****

10. What group did Box Tops' leader Alex Chilton form in the early '70s ?
>   a. Alive & Kicking
>   b. Big Star
>   c. Hotlegs

11. From what country did Blue Öyster Cult originate ?
           a. Denmark
           b. Germany
           c. the U.S.

****

12. Of the nine #1 hits by Paul McCartney (as a solo, in a
    duet, and with Wings), which stayed on top for the
    longest time ?
           a. *Ebony & Ivory*
           b. *Silly Love Songs*
           c. *Say Say Say*

****

13. What was Frank Zappa's only Top 40 hit ?
           a. *Dancin' Fool*
           b. *Burnt Weeny Sandwich*
           c. *Valley Girl*

****

14. The Allman Brothers Band was the first group to record
    under a new Atlantic record label. What was the name
    of the label ?
           a. Arista
           b. Capricorn
           c. Chrysalis

****

15. From what did Deep Purple derive their name ?
           a. from a Boris Karloff thriller
           b. from a 1963 hit song
           c. from their favorite color

16. What was unique about the titles of Chicago's albums ?
    a. Each subsequent album title began with a different letter.
    b. They were all drawn by a spray-paint master.
    c. Each was numbered.

****

17. Todd Rundgren's most successful single was his 1973
    release of which song recorded by his band, Nazz, in
    1969 ?
    a. *I Saw the Light*
    b. *Hello It's Me*
    c. *We Gotta Get You a Woman*

****

18. Which of the following played lead guitar on the
    Bill Withers hit *Ain't No Sunshine* ?
    a. Eddie Van Halen
    b. Jose Feliciano
    c. Stephen Stills

****

19. What nickname accompanied David Bowie in the '70s ?
    a. the Thin White Duke
    b. the Crossfire Prince
    c. Major Tom

****

20. Who wrote Manfred Mann's Earth Band's *Blinded By
    the Light,* co-wrote Patti Smith's *Because the Night,*
    and wrote the Pointer Sisters' *Fire* ?
    a. Jackson Browne
    b. Bruce Springsteen
    c. Barry Manilow

HARDER QUESTIONS: Worth 2 points each — 4 points if you can answer the question without the three choices !
****

1. After which famed blues singer (and his saxophonist) did he select the name Elton John ?
    a. John Mayall
    b. Long John Baldry
    c. Johnny Mack

****

2. Who said the following: "I'm not too good at pulling strings — 12 is my maximum; 6 is my specialty."
    a. Keith Richards
    b. Eddie Van Halen
    c. Eric Clapton

****

3. What Electric Light Orchestra song was a remake of a minor hit by their earlier incarnation, the Move ?
    a. *Telephone Line*
    b. *Don't Bring Me Down*
    c. *Do Ya*

****

4. From what did the British band Supertramp get its name ?
    a. a dredging rig
    b. a book
    c. the movies *Superman* and *Lady & the Tramp*

****

5. Who said the following during a British performance: "Those in the cheaper seats, clap. The rest of you, rattle your jewelry."
    a. John Lennon
    b. Frank Zappa
    c. Elton John

ANSWERS

****

1. b. Hamilton, Joe Frank & Reynolds (Dan Hamilton; Joe Frank Carollo; and Tom Reynolds)
2. c. Each member released a solo album (dressed up in "Kiss" attire).
3. a. *Take it Easy*
4. b. Aerosmith
5. c. the Amboy Dukes (who recorded *Journey to the Center of the Mind* in 1968)
6. a. *Money*
7. a. 1964
8. b. *Fame*
9. c. the Nazz (Todd Rundgren's already-named group Nazz had no affiliation with Cooper)
10. b. Big Star
11. c. the U.S. (The Ö was added for international appeal.)
12. a. *Ebony & Ivory* (with Stevie Wonder, #1 for seven weeks, one more than *Say, Say, Say,* his duet with Michael Jackson)
13. c. *Valley Girl* (featuring daughter Moon Unit)
14. b. Capricorn
15. b. from the 1963 hit *Deep Purple* by Nino Tempo & April Stevens
16. c. Each was numbered (from Chicago III to Chicago 19).
17. b. *Hello It's Me* (which peaked at #5 in December)
18. c. Stephen Stills
19. a. the Thin White Duke
20. b. Bruce Springsteen

****

HARDER QUESTIONS--Answers

1. b. Long John Baldry (the first name came from Baldry's saxophonist, Elton Dean)
2. a. Keith Richards
3. c. *Do Ya* (which reached #24 in 1977)
4. b. the 1910 book *The Autobiography of a Supertramp,* by W. H. Davies
5. a. John Lennon

1. What two British bands was English-born Peter
   Frampton in during the late '60s ?
   > a. the Herd and Humble Pie
   > b. the Fourmost and Blind Faith
   > c. the Shindogs and Spooky Tooth

****

2. Why was Foreigner a suitable name for the group ?
   > a. because they liked to tour overseas
   > b. because the name fit their new music style
   > c. because the members were from both the United States
   >   and England

****

3. Which character did Elton John play in the Who's 1975
   film version of the classic *Tommy* ?
   > a. Tommy's dad
   > b. the Pinball Wizard
   > c. Tommy

****

4. Why did Kansas change their name from White Clover ?
   > a. They wanted a name that avoided racial association.
   > b. Another local group was already called White Clover.
   > c. The band members were all from Kansas.

****

5. What was John Lennon's last single to reach the Top 5
   in the U.S. music charts ?
   > a. *Woman*
   > b. *Whatever Gets You Through the Night*
   > c. *(Just Like) Starting Over*

6. What #1 song in the '60s did Grand Funk cover and take to the top of the charts in the '70s ?

      a. *Some Kind of Wonderful*

      b. *The Loco-Motion*

      c. *Walk Like a Man*

****

7. Which Pink Floyd album defied gravity by staying on the album charts for seventeen years ?!

      a. *The Wall*

      b. *Dark Side of the Moon*

      c. *Ummagumma*

****

8. On what label did Bad Company record all their U.S. hits ?

      a. A&M

      b. I.R.S.

      c. Swan Song

****

9. What George Harrison hit became the subject of a lawsuit over copyright infringement in the mid-'70s ?

      a. *My Sweet Lord*

      b. *Give Me Love (Give Me Peace on Earth)*

      c. *What Is Life*

****

10. Besides *A Horse With No Name,* what other America hit reached #1 ?

      a. *Tin Man*

      b. *You Can Do Magic*

      c. *Sister Golden Hair*

11. Which of the the following is a graduate of the
New York City Police Academy ?
>   a. Meat Loaf
>   b. Eddie Money
>   c. Bruce Springsteen

****

12. Whose sponsorship of the group helped Supertramp
get their start ?
>   a. the British government
>   b. a young millionaire
>   c. an oil company

****

13. What was Jackson Browne's highest–charting single ?
>   a. *Somebody's Baby*
>   b. *Doctor My Eyes*
>   c. *Running on Empty*

****

14. What prompted the band to call themselves "Boston" ?
>   a. Although from Chicago, they couldn't use that name —
>   it was already taken — so they selected another city name.
>   b. The members were all from Boston.
>   c. They were inspired by the Standell's song *Dirty Water,*
>   a tribute to Boston.

****

15. Which group is being referred to with the comment
that their "audience wasn't the sensitive crowd. It was
the guy who just dropped three downs, swigged a
bottle of Boone's Farm, and did a lot of hanging out".
>   a. Supertramp
>   b. Steve Miller Band
>   c. Grand Funk Railroad

16. Before they became 10cc, the group (then a trio, later to add a fourth member and become 10cc) had a Top 40 U.S. Hit (Top 5 in the U.K). What was this hit ?
>   a. *Telstar*
>   b. *Psychotic Reaction*
>   c. *Neanderthal Man*

****

17. Which #1 U.S. hit by Rod Stewart was generally banned in the U.K. ?
>   a. *Tonight's the Night (Gonna Be Alright)*
>   b. *Da Ya Think I'm Sexy*
>   c. *Hot Legs*

****

18. How did the members of Kiss first meet ?
>   a. by responding to a newspaper ad
>   b. in a musical play dress rehearsal
>   c. at Coney Island

****

19. Foreigner's *I Want to Know What Love Is* spent two weeks in the #1 position. What Foreigner song spent ten weeks in the #2 position three years earlier ?
>   a. *Hot Blooded*
>   b. *Double Vision*
>   c. *Waiting For a Girl Like You*

****

20. What label did Led Zeppelin form in 1974 ?
>   a. Big Tree
>   b. Swan Song
>   c. Casablanca

HARDER QUESTIONS: Worth 2 points each — 4 points if you can answer the question without the three choices !
****

1. In what 1970 movie soundtrack did Pink Floyd include three songs ?
    a. *Jesus Christ Superstar*
    b. *Zabriskie Point*
    c. *Butch Cassidy & the Sundance Kid*
****

2. Which band was declared by the *Guinness Book of World Records* in 1976 to be the loudest performing band in the world ?
    a. the Rolling Stones
    b. the Who
    c. Black Sabbath
****

3. Who was *Billboard Magazine* referring to when they said that he "could have a big following when he finds his own style" ?
    a. Bruce Springsteen
    b. Bob Seger
    c. Bob Dylan
****

4. In what country was Queen's leader Freddie Mercury born ?
    a. Tanzania
    b. Austria
    c. Australia
****

5. From what college did Boston leader Tom Scholz graduate ?
    a. Boston College
    b. M.I.T.
    c. Juilliard

ANSWERS

****

1. a. the Herd and Humble Pie
2. c. because the members were from both the United States and England
3. b. the Pinball Wizard
4. c. The band members were all from Kansas.
5. a. *Woman*
6. b. *The Loco-Motion* (#1 hit in 1962 for Little Eva)
7. b. *Dark Side of the Moon* (which has sold more than 12 million copies!)
8. c. Swan Song, owned by Led Zeppelin
9. a. *My Sweet Lord* (due to its similarity to the Chiffons' hit *He's So Fine* . . . seriously ?!)
10. c. *Sister Golden Hair*
11. b. Eddie Money
12. b. a young Dutch millionaire, Stanley Miesegaes
13. a. *Somebody's Baby* (from the soundtrack of *Fast Times at Ridgemont High* . . . it reached #7)
14. b. The members were all from Boston.
15. c. Grand Funk Railroad
16. c. *Neanderthal Man* (as Hotlegs)
17. a. *Tonight's the Night (Gonna Be Alright)* because of its seductive, deflowering lyrics
18. a. by responding to a newspaper ad
19. c. *Waiting For a Girl Like You* (which got upstaged by Olivia Newton-John's *Physical* for most of its reign in 1981)
20. b. Swan Song

****

HARDER QUESTIONS--Answers

1. b. *Zabriskie Point*
2. b. the Who (whose 1976 performance measured 120 decibels)
3. c. Bob Dylan
4. a. Tanzania (as Frederick Bulsara)
5. b. M.I.T. (a master's degree in mechanical engineering)

1. Which of the following musicians has an advanced degree in Mathematics from prestigious Columbia University ?

        a. Billy Joel
        b. Art Garfunkel
        c. Jimmy Buffett

****

2. Who had the lead role in the movie *Tommy* ?

        a. Elton John
        b. Roger Daltry
        c. David Bowie

****

3. Of the three ZZ Top members, which one didn't sport a long beard ?

        a. Billy Gibbons
        b. Dusty Hill
        c. Frank Beard

****

4. Which of the following was Supertramp's highest-charting single ?

        a. *Give a Little Bit*
        b. *Take the Long Way Home*
        c. *The Logical Song*

****

5. What 1971 movie did Frank Zappa make as a fictionalized "documentary" of his band ?

        a. *200 Motels*
        b. *Crackers*
        c. *Uncle Meat*

6. In what 1970 film did Mick Jagger act as a lipstick-
wearing, retired rock star ?
>   a. *Gimme Shelter*
>   b. *Performance*
>   c. *It's Only Rock 'n' Roll*

****

7. What is a "Steely Dan" ?
>   a. a reinforced support beam,
>   used in commercial buildings
>   b. a type of marble
>   c. a steam-powered dildo

****

8. How long is the tongue of Kiss leader Gene Simmons ?
>   a. 4 inches
>   b. 7 inches
>   c. 12 inches

****

9. What was the inspiration behind *Jet* ?
>   a. Paul McCartney's pet
>   b. a recent love gone sour
>   c. the British Concorde

****

10. Which of the following groups did <u>not</u> contribute any
members to the Eagles ?
>   a. Poco
>   b. Flying Burrito Brothers
>   c. America

11. From what country did Air Supply originate ?

> a. Sweden
> b. Australia
> c. England

****

12. What tribute to the American way of life was John Cougar Mellencamp's only #1 hit ?

> a. *Jack & Diane*
> b. *R.O.C.K. In the U.S.A.*
> c. *Pink Houses*

****

13. What actress did Eddie Van Halen marry in 1981 ?

> a. Valerie Bertinelli
> b. Vanna White
> c. Susan Sarandon

****

14. What major rock figure did Tom Petty & the Heartbreakers back up during 1986–1987 ?

> a. Bob Dylan
> b. Bob Seger
> c. Richard Marx

****

15. *Open Arms* was Journey's biggest single, charting at #2 for six weeks. What song kept it from reaching the #1 spot ?

> a. *Centerfold*
> b. *Ebony & Ivory*
> c. *I Love Rock 'N Roll*

16. What religious affiliation includes '70s rock stars Seals & Crofts ?

        a. Christian Science

        b. Baha'i Faith

        c. Jehovah's Witness

****

17. In which city were all the original members of Cheap Trick born ?

        a. Rockford, Illinois

        b. Sydney, Australia

        c. London, England

****

18. What was Eric Clapton's only #1 hit in the '70s and '80s ?

        a. *Lay Down Sally*

        b. *Layla*

        c. *I Shot the Sheriff*

****

19. Bruce Springsteen never had a U.S. #1 hit single. Which song reached #2 ?

        a. *Born In the U.S.A.*

        b. *Dancing in the Dark*

        c. *Hungry Heart*

****

20. For what album did Bob Seger win "Best Rock Performance" at the 1981 Grammy Awards ?

        a. *Stranger in Town*

        b. *Night Moves*

        c. *Against the Wind*

HARDER QUESTIONS: Worth 2 points each — 4 points if you can answer the question without the three choices !

****

1. REO Speedwagon took their name from Ransom Eli Olds. Who was he ?

      a. a 1920s blues singer

      b. the father of the Oldsmobile Corporation

      c. Kevin Cronin's great-grandfather

****

2. Blondie's Deborah Harry first sang in a late-'60s folk-rock band that was named after a book about small animals. What was the name of this group ?

      a. Ben & the Rodents

      b. Willard

      c. Wind in the Willows

****

3. Who inspired the name for the Police ?

      a. Randy California, in his song *1984*

      b. Stewart Copeland's father

      c. George Harrison

****

4. Bruce Springsteen rejected a $12 million offer to promote which company ?

      a. Chrysler

      b. Budweiser

      c. Exxon

****

5. The manager of which British rock megastar first signed John Cougar to a record contract ?

      a. Elton John

      b. Rod Stewart

      c. David Bowie

ANSWERS

****

1. b. Art Garfunkel
2. b. Roger Daltry
3. c. Frank Beard
4. c. *The Logical Song* (which reached #6 in 1979)
5. a. *200 Motels* (in which Turtles founders and Zappa back-up singers Howard Kaylan and Mark Volman appeared)
6. b. *Performance*
7. c. a steam-powered dildo (as featured in William Burroughs' novel *Naked Lunch*)
8. b. 7 inches (2 inches longer than the average length)
9. a. Paul McCartney's pet (a Labrador pup)
10. c. America
11. b. Australia
12. a. *Jack & Diane* (#1 for four weeks in 1982)
13. a. Valerie Bertinelli
14. a. Bob Dylan
15. c. *I Love Rock 'N Roll* (by Joan Jett & the Blackhearts, which spent seven weeks on top in 1982)
16. b. Baha'i Faith
17. a. Rockford, Illinois
18. c. *I Shot the Sheriff* (written by Bob Marley)
19. b. *Dancing in the Dark* (#2 for four weeks)
20. c. *Against the Wind*

****

HARDER QUESTIONS--Answers

1. b. the father of the Oldsmobile Corporation (and builder of the fire truck that became the group's namesake)
2. c. Wind in the Willows (from the book *Wind in the Willows* by Kenneth Graham)
3. b. Stewart Copeland's father (who worked for the CIA and taught him the "tricks of the trade")
4. a. Chrysler (which sought *Born in the U.S.A.* for their commercials)
5. c. David Bowie (whose manager, Tony DeFries, was contacted by John Mellencamp—a long-time fan of David Bowie. DeFries suggested the name "Johnny Cougar," though the young rocker added his true last name—Mellencamp—in 1983.)

1. What was Billy Idol's birth name ?
   a. Chad Arthur
   b. Robert Grundy
   c. William Broad

****

2. From what 1980 film did Electric Light Orchestra score three Top Twenty hits, including the title track ?
   a. *The Gambler*
   b. *Xanadu*
   c. *Grease*

****

3. Which Police album reigned supreme for seventeen weeks and spawned a #1 single ?
   a. *Syncronicity*
   b. *Zenyatta Mondatta*
   c. *Ghost in the Machine*

****

4. What nickname has stuck with Bruce Springsteen through the years ?
   a. the Asbury Prince
   b. the Gunslinger
   c. the Boss

****

5. With whom did original Heart lead singer Ann Wilson duet in 1984 in a Top 10 hit ?
   a. Mike Reno
   b. Michael McDonald
   c. Joe Cocker

6. *Keep on Loving You* was REO Speedwagon's first #1 hit. What was their other #1 song ?

        a. *Can't Fight This Feeling*
        b. *Take It On the Run*
        c. *Keep the Fire Burnin'*

****

7. Cherilyn Sarkisian LaPierre was the real (birth) name for which of the following ?

        a. Cheryl Crow
        b. Cher
        c. Madonna

****

8. What accolade did the Cars receive in 1979 ?

    a. Grammy Award for "Song of the the Year"
    b. Elektra Records' "Elektric Rock" award
    c. Rolling Stone Magazine's "Best New Band of the Year"

****

9. From what country did Men at Work originate ?

        a. England
        b. South Africa
        c. Australia

****

10. For what 1980 movie did Queen write and provide the soundtrack ?

        a. *Flash Gordon*
        b. *Urban Cowboy*
        c. *One-Trick Pony*

11. After what were Dexys Midnight Runners named ?
   a. dexedrine
   b. the manager's pet hamster
   c. an early–'40s cowboy movie

****

12. In what movie did Survivor's #1 hit *Eye of the Tiger* appear ?
   a. *An Officer & A Gentleman*
   b. *Rocky III*
   c. *The Karate Kid Part II*

****

13. How many Grammy awards did Toto win in 1983 ?
   a. two
   b. three
   c. six

****

14. What Queen single not only topped the U.S. rock charts but also hit #2 on the Rhythm & Blues charts as well ?
   a. *Crazy Little Thing Called Love*
   b. *Another One Bites the Dust*
   c. *We Will Rock You*

****

15. *Hi Fidelity* broke REO Speedwagon into the top of the album charts and included such hits as *Keep on Loving You* and *Take It on the Run.* Which album was this for the band ?
   a. their first
   b. their third
   c. their eleventh

16. What was the name of Bruce Springsteen's long-running backup group ?
> a. the Sonic Boom
> b. the E Street Band
> c. the Asbury Dukes

****

17. Which Air Supply song was their only one to reach #1 ?
> a. *The One That You Love*
> b. *Lost in Love*
> c. *All Out of Love*

****

18. With whom did David Bowie sing a Christmas duet in 1982 ?
> a. George Burns
> b. Luciano Pavorotti
> c. Bing Crosby

****

19. Of their six #1 hits, which one stayed on top the longest for Daryl Hall & John Oates ?
> a. *Maneater*
> b. *Kiss on My List*
> c. *Rich Girl*

****

20. Which Chicago member scored two solo #1 hits in 1986 ?
> a. Robert Lamm
> b. Peter Cetera
> c. Terry Kath

HARDER QUESTIONS: Worth 2 points each — 4 points if you can answer the question without the three choices !

****

1. What famous early '60s star did Bruce Springsteen produce during the early '80s ?

      a. Ben E. King

      b. Roy Orbison

      c. Gary U.S. Bonds

****

2. What motivated Police singer/bass guitarist Gordon Sumner to adopt the nickname "Sting" ?

      a. Andy Summers' pet snake

      b. a favorite black–and–yellow jersey

      c. his raspy voice

****

3. Styx was originally known as TW4. Why did they use this abbreviation rather than the name the initials stood for ?

      a. to avoid confusion with the group the Trade Winds

      b. to satisfy angry Trans World Airlines lawyers

      c. to capitalize on the British success of the DC5

****

4. Who made the following comment during a concert: "Blind faith . . . is a dangerous thing, whether it's your girlfriend . . . or your government".

      a. David Crosby

      b. Bruce Springsteen

      c. Bob Dylan

****

5. What product did the Police promote in a 1978 television ad ?

      a. *Levi's* jeans

      b. *Nike* shoes

      c. *Wrigley's* Gum

ANSWERS

1. c. William Broad
2. b. *Xanadu* (ELO backed Olivia Newton-John on the soundtrack hit)
3. a. *Syncronicity,* which included the single *Every Breath You Take* (#1 for eight weeks)
4. c. the Boss
5. a. Mike Reno (Loverboy lead singer—in *Almost Paradise,* the love theme from *Footloose*)
6. a. *Can't Fight This Feeling* (which topped the charts for three weeks in 1985)
7. b. Cher
8. c. *Rolling Stones'* "Best New Band of the Year"
9. c. Australia
10. a. *Flash Gordon*
11. a. dexedrine, a widely used "upper"
12. b. *Rocky III*
13. c. six (including Record and Album of the Year)
14. b. *Another One Bites the Dust*
15. c. their eleventh (Formed in 1968, the band titled their tenth album *A Decade of Rock 'n' Roll,* and it featured ten years of their music. Overnight success doesn't always come early!)
16. b. the E Street Band
17. a. *The One That You Love*
18. c. Bing Crosby (in the medley *Peace on Earth/Little Drummer Boy*)
19. a. *Maneater* (#1 for four weeks in 1982)
20. b. Peter Cetera *(Glory of Love* and *The Next Time I Fall,* with Amy Grant)

HARDER QUESTIONS--Answers

1. c. Gary U.S. Bonds
2. b. a favorite black-and-yellow jersey
3. a. to avoid confusion with the group the Trade Winds (The Styx members were originally called the Tradewinds when they formed in 1964, but with the 1965 hit *New York's a Lonely Town* by the New York group Trade Winds, they elected to avoid any possible future confusion.)
4. b. Bruce Springsteen
5. c. *Wrigley's* Gum (they appeared in a *Wrigley's* chewing gum ad)

1. For what pop megastar did Eddie Van Halen contribute a guitar solo ?
>   a. Michael Jackson
>   b. Paul Simon
>   c. Madonna

****

2. Which famous British rocker added vocals — and his own melody — into Dire Straits' biggest hit, *Money for Nothing* ?
>   a. Sting
>   b. Elton John
>   c. Billy Idol

****

3. Which of the following was <u>not</u> a hit from Men At Work's first album ?
>   a. *Overkill*
>   b. *Who Can It Be Now*
>   c. *Down Under*

****

4. In what city was Journey formed ?
>   a. London
>   b. New York City
>   c. San Francisco

****

5. Blondie had four #1 hits. Which one was #1 for the longest period of time ?
>   a. *Call Me*
>   b. *Heart of Glass*
>   c. *Rapture*

6. What was Cheap Trick's only #1 hit ?

    a. *I Want You to Want Me*

    b. *The Flame*

    c. *Don't Be Cruel*

****

7. Who was the <u>original</u> lead singer of Genesis ?

    a. Denny Laine

    b. Peter Gabriel

    c. Phil Collins

****

8. In what TV soap opera did Rick Springfield have a regular role ?

    a. *As The World Turns*

    b. *The Guiding Light*

    c. *General Hospital*

****

9. What Top 5 Survivor hit came from the movie *Rocky IV* ?

    a. *I Can't Hold Back*

    b. *The Search is Over*

    c. *Burning Heart*

****

10. What was the name of Bob Seger's band during the time of *Ramblin' Gamblin' Man* ?

    a. Bob Seger & the Last Heard

    b. Bob Seger System

    c. the Quaker City Boys

11. Which rock group did Dire Straits tour with during their first U.K. gig ?
    a. the Rolling Stones
    b. the Clash
    c. Talking Heads

****

12. What London-based punk band did Billy Idol lead in the late '70s ?
    a. Generation X
    b. Sex Pistols
    c. Roxy Music

****

13. Who replaced lead singer David Lee Roth shortly after his departure from Van Halen ?
    a. Jon Bon Jovi
    b. Sammy Hagar
    c. Alex Van Halen

****

14. What recreational activity is Ted Nugent well-known for ?
    a. hunting
    b. hang-gliding
    c. mountain climbing

****

15. What was the first hit for Tom Petty & the Heartbreakers to reach the Top 10 in the singles chart?
    a. *The Waiting*
    b. *Refugee*
    c. *Don't Do Me Like That*

16. Men At Work's *Business As Usual* album topped the U.S. charts for fifteen weeks, surpassing by three weeks the previous highest-ranking debut album. Who had held the previous record ?

    a. the Beatles

    b. the Supremes

    c. the Monkees

****

17. How did Queen's Freddie Mercury die ?

    a. from a heart attack

    b. from AIDS

    c. he was hit by a truck

****

18. What mid-'80s group did original Genesis guitarist Mike Rutherford form ?

    a. Survivor

    b. Wham!

    c. Mike + the Mechanics

****

19. Which of the following hits did Bruce Springsteen <u>not</u> write ?

    a. *Island Girl* (Elton John hit)

    b. *Fire* (Pointer Sisters hit)

    c. *Blinded By the Light* (Manfred Mann's Earth Band hit)

****

20. The origin of the group name Toto has been an enduring mystery. Which of the following was <u>not</u> a reason for the band's choice of their name ?

a. It was named after a comet.

b. It was inspired by *The Wizard of Oz.*

c. It came from lead singer Bobby Kimball's original last name, Toteaux.

1. Which of the following was <u>not</u> a former band name for the members of Cheap Trick ?

      a. Fuse

      b. Chicken Funk

      c. Sick Man of Europe

****

2. "Heart" was shortened from their previous name. What was it ?

      a. Broken Heart

      b. White Heart

      c. Heart & Soul

****

3. In what movie did the Pretenders' biggest hit, *Back on the Chain Gang,* appear ?

      a. *The Goonies*

      b. *The King of Comedy*

      c. *Two of a Kind*

****

4. Which of the following was <u>not</u> an occupation of vocalist Mark Knopfler before he formed Dire Straits ?

      a. journalist

      b. social worker

      c. part-time teacher

****

5. Who made this comment: "If it hadn't been for Elvis [Presley], I'd probably be driving a snowplow in Minneapolis."

      a. Bob Seger

      b. Bruce Springsteen

      c. Prince

ANSWERS

****

1. a. Michael Jackson (in the #1 song *Beat It*)
2. a. Sting (who interjected the melody of *Don't Stand So Close to Me* to the words "I Want My MTV")
3. a. *Overkill*
4. c. San Francisco
5. a. *Call Me* (#1 for six weeks)
6. b. *The Flame* (in 1988)
7. b. Peter Gabriel (Phil Collins sang lead in the band's later hits)
8. c. *General Hospital* (he played Noah Drake)
9. c. *Burning Heart*
10. b. Bob Seger System
11. c. Talking Heads
12. a. Generation X (from 1977 to 1981)
13. b. Sammy Hagar (lead singer of lesser-known '80s band Montrose)
14. a. hunting
15. c. *Don't Do Me Like That*
16. c. the Monkees (with their 1967 debut album *The Monkees*)
17. b. from AIDS (1991)
18. c. Mike + the Mechanics
19. a. *Island Girl*
20. a. Though some sources dispute Bobby Kimball's last name as Toteaux, Toto was definitely not a comet.

****

HARDER QUESTIONS--Answers

1. b. Chicken Funk
2. b. White Heart
3. b. *The King of Comedy*
4. b. social worker
5. c. Prince

Made in the USA
Lexington, KY
02 September 2018